MOTIVATIONAL DIMENSIONS IN SOCIAL MOVEMENTS
AND CONTENTIOUS COLLECTIVE ACTION

Motivational Dimensions in Social Movements and Contentious Collective Action

MAURICE PINARD

McGill-Queen's University Press

Montreal & Kingston • London • Ithaca

ISBN 978-0-7735-3865-8 (cloth)
ISBN 978-0-7735-3866-5 (paper)

Legal deposit third quarter 2011
Bibliothèque nationale du Québec

Printed in Canada on acid-free paper that is 100% ancient forest free (100% post-consumer recycled), processed chlorine free

McGill-Queen's University Press acknowledges the support of the Canada Council for the Arts for our publishing program. We also acknowledge the financial support of the Government of Canada through the Canada Book Fund for our publishing activities.

Library and Archives Canada Cataloguing in Publication Data

Pinard, Maurice, 1929–
   Motivational dimensions in social movements and contentious collective action / Maurice Pinard.

Includes bibliographical references and index.
ISBN 978-0-7735-3865-8 (bound). – ISBN 978-0-7735-3866-5 (pbk.)

1. Social movements – Psychological aspects. 2. Social action – Psychological aspects. 3. Motivation (Psychology) – Social aspects. I. Title.

HM881.P55 2011   303.48'4   C2011-901259-6

Typeset by Jay Tee Graphics Ltd. in 10/13 Sabon

Contents

Preface

The basic concern of this book is to re-examine and synthesize in a new model the multiple dimensions of motivation that studies of social movements and of other forms of contentious collective action ought to incorporate. On the whole and but for a few exceptions, the motivational paradigms adopted in the general approaches to such collective action have changed substantially over the years, but they have always been very partial, at least in the dominant theories. In addition, the importance attached to motivational factors in explaining contentious action has substantially decreased over time, these factors becoming increasingly neglected in favour of structural factors, albeit also very important, such as organization, resources, opportunities, and mobilization.

Thus while the early narrow motivational perspectives prevailing in the study of collective behaviour and social movements focused mainly on the role of discontents and deprivations, subsequent perspectives, such as those found in the resource mobilization and political process or contentious politics approaches, disregarded such internal motives in favour of equally narrow considerations of general interests as collective incentives and of selective incentives. And even such considerations became very secondary to those concerning other determinants of collective action.

To be sure, during recent decades, while the new theoretical paradigms continued to prevail, more sophisticated cultural and social psychological perspectives in the field emerged rather independently, but with important and relevant focus on motivational concerns. These motivational views, however, have all too often failed to be taken seriously by general theorists and to be properly incorporated into the latter's frameworks, and scholars guided in their empirical research by such general frameworks often uncritically followed suit, ignoring motivational components altogether.

This book is clearly set within the new social psychology of collective action. Its basic premise rests on the conviction that there are valid elements in both early and contemporary motivational perspectives, as well as in other writings. But even the new approaches tended to ignore others, when not negating their relevance, so that each leaves much to be desired. I believe that together with the addition of other components, a new synthesis can be elaborated that will, I hope, lead to the development of worthwhile new motivational perspectives.

The paths toward that goal will be the following ones. In chapter 1, a critical examination of the partial – if at all present – models of motivation found over time in major theoretical approaches will be reviewed, with a concentration on their respective claims regarding the role of objective deprivations and felt grievances. The frequent confusions regarding the nature and the conditions of their effects, which are not invariant, will have to be lifted. In addition the role attributed to grievances in recent contributions in the social psychology of contentious action, particularly in the literature bearing on framing processes and on the role of emotions, will also be acknowledged.

But it is on empirical evidence, all too often disregarded or misrepresented, that the validity of conflicting claims regarding the impact of grievances ultimately rests. The evidence will be reviewed in detail, and the controversies generated by apparently conflicting results will be critically examined in chapter 2, in an effort to set the record straight. This will be followed in chapter 3 by a discussion of the serious methodological problems often at the source of such disputes, such as data and measurement problems, as well as more general analytical flaws in research designs.

In chapter 4, attention will then turn to other, often neglected, motivational components. First, simple aspirations as internal motives that could possibly be alternatives to grievances will be considered. Again, controversies regarding their impact will have to be cleared up. This will be followed by an examination of the main motivational components considered in contemporary theories, that is, external incentives, both collective and selective; in particular the conditions of their relevance and their interaction with grievances will be examined. The presumed impact of some cultural dimensions, such as ideology, collective identity, and solidarity, will then be discussed, leading to the conclusion that in contentious action a third specific internal motive, felt moral obligations, must be taken into account. Finally, expectancy of success, a too often neglected motivational component, will be presented as a key determinant.

This will open the way for the presentation in chapter 5 of a general model of motivation. It was inspired by John Atkinson's achievement motivation theory, which posits that, when individual action is concerned, three elements are necessary, that is, an internal motive to reach a goal, the external incentive value of that goal, and the strength of the expectancy of success in reaching it. This theory will appropriately be modified to apply to collective rather than individual action and to incorporate, in a synthesis, the components found relevant in the discussions of previous chapters. In particular it will distinguish three possible internal motives, that is, grievances and attending emotions, aspirations, and moral obligations, and two alternative incentives, collective and selective, as well as the expectancy of success. Particular attention will be paid to the very different ways in which these components combine under different conditions. This will be followed by a set of hypotheses concerning other secondary variations in motivational patterns according to different contexts of contentious collective action.

Finally, chapter 6 will turn from a consideration of motivation as an independent variable affecting other dimensions of collective action to considering it as the dependent variable, asking in particular what are the impacts of two basic cultural dimensions, framing activities and collective identities, on one or the other dimension of motivation. All in all my hope is that my theoretical efforts will make some worthwhile contributions to a better understanding of the role of motivation in contentious mobilization.

In these efforts, I gained a lot from the advice, criticisms, and encouragements of many colleagues. I am very grateful to the many who, over the years, graciously offered their suggestions on one draft or another of the writings leading to this book. Acknowledgments are made to Sam Clark, William Gamson, Richard Hamilton, Matthew Lange, Patricia LeCavalier, Anthony Oberschall, Daniele Petrosino, James Rule, Michael Smith, Suzanne Staggenborg, James Wood, Mayer Zald, and Dingxin Zhao. I particularly profited from access to unpublished material and from frequent discussions and comments with a long-time friend and colleague, Donald Von Eschen, who was always available to let me bounce new ideas against his vast knowledge and wise critical assessment of our field. During the final stages in the production of this work, the unfailing research assistance of France-Pascale Ménard was really most helpful. So were the contributions from the personnel of McGill-Queen's University Press, especially those of Philip Cercone, executive director, Joan McGilvray, coordinating editor, and Jessica Howarth, editorial assistant.

Finally, but not least, I have accumulated a very special debt of gratitude toward Minola and Pierre for their constant forbearance and support in this as well as in my other professional activities.

MOTIVATIONAL DIMENSIONS IN SOCIAL MOVEMENTS AND CONTENTIOUS COLLECTIVE ACTION

1

Approaches to Motivation in the Social Movement Literature

One of the fundamental questions in the study of social movements and other forms of contentious collective action concerns the motivation of people attracted to such action. Briefly, and concretely, the questions asked are, first, what motivates the members of a group to hold favourable, indifferent, or unfavourable *opinions* towards the goals of various forms of collective action and towards the responses of their opponents? Second, what motivates them to *participate* in such actions or movements, that is, to make small or large contributions of various resources (labour power, money, time, material goods, votes, etc.) useful for the pursuit of such goals? And third, how do such motivations influence the emergence, development, persistence, or decline of social movements?

When one looks at answers previously provided to such questions in the social movement literature, one is soon enmeshed in a series of intense controversies regarding not only the validity of this or that theory of motivation but even the importance or necessity of paying much attention to the development of such a theory in the first place.

While traditionally scholars had argued that some forms of objective deprivations or felt grievances constituted the essential internal motives for the emergence of and participation in all types of collective behaviour and social movements, scholars from alternative theoretical approaches that were developed during the 1970s and beyond largely rejected such a position, insisting instead that external incentives of some sorts – not deprivations – had to be considered as the essential motivating forces. It was only during the 1980s that grievance arguments did occasionally reappear as a reaction against such claims.

To be sure the controversies over the role of deprivations and grievances have since lost their intensity. But this is in part because the problem is simply disregarded by a number of scholars and silence about the issue prevails among many. The controversial arguments must be reconsidered, and contentious claims need to be adjudicated. Above all in that process, other motivational components will emerge as also important. To attend to all of this a detailed review of previous perspectives is necessary.

Such a review will lead to a series of criticisms of opposite approaches as a first step toward the ultimate development of a new multidimensional and multiplicative model of motivation. This model, originally inspired by Atkinson's (1964) theory of achievement motivation, will consider the internal motives pushing one to participate in collective action. That first component will include three potential elements, deprivations or felt grievances, but also simple aspirations for goods one does not feel deprived of, and moral obligations, the sense that it is one's duty to make some contribution to the collective action. The second component will consider the external incentives pulling one towards such action and will include two elements, the collective goods or incentives pursued and the personal rewards and costs or selective incentives encountered in that process. Finally, a third component, expectancy of success in reaching the immediate or distant goals of the action, will be included.

Let me state from the beginning that one of the basic hypotheses in this first chapter is that deprivations and grievances are among the most important motivational components that need to be considered in the analysis of contentious collective action.

But first some immediately relevant definitions. Social movements have been defined in many different ways. Writers in the dominant political process approach view social movements as sustained and organized public collective action aimed at making claims involving political authorities. While seen as relevant, many have proposed broader definitions, arguing, among other things, that social movements also include less public conflicts with authorities in non-political institutions or involving larger cultural as well as political challenges. Ethnopolitical, women's, peace, and ecological movements are well-known examples of all such social movements. In addition, other forms of contentious collective action must also be considered, such as occasional and barely organized collective protests not linked to social movements but also engaged in challenging authority systems or normative arrangements. Examples of these include sudden demonstrations, petitions, boycotts, violent outbursts, and similar phenomena.

Objective deprivations are defined as disadvantageous conditions or morally objectionable situations, actual or anticipated, as perceived individually and collectively by members of a social group. The term *felt grievances* refers to experienced sentiments of discontent about such actual or anticipated conditions or situations evaluated as unjust or illegitimate and attributable to some responsible agents. In what follows, *deprivations* will refer to the *objective* conditions, while the term *grievances* will imply *felt* sentiments.[1] Deprivations and grievances are motives of highly variable severity and intensity, respectively. When they are only anticipated, they will constitute subcategories identified as objective or felt *threats*. Although not always clearly differentiated in the literature, these concepts have until recently been dominant in analyses of contentious action, at least when problems of internal motivation have been at all considered; they will therefore constitute the dimensions that will mainly retain our attention in large sections of this book. However, since the 1990s, in some social-psychological approaches, it has been rightly argued that another dimension, *emotions,* ought to receive much greater attention than it gets. This will be done in subsequent sections and in the ultimate model developed, with emotions defined as sentiments or feelings generated as reactions to events or resulting from affective bonds. Although conceptually very close to grievances, emotions, varying in intensity, will be kept analytically distinct, and they will enter our propositions jointly as *grievances/emotions* motives.

If deprivations, grievances, and emotions, together with other motivational components, turn out to be important dimensions of collective action, one can expect them to affect other structural and cultural dimensions of such action. Thus the amount and type of resources mobilized will largely depend on the grievances and other motives of potential contributors. Such motivations will also affect the definitions and redefinitions of the goals pursued and of the beliefs and ideologies developed, the scope of organization within contending groups, and the tactics and strategies they adopt, as well as the successes and failures of their action. Reversed effects between such dimensions and motivation are of course also possible. Some authors may want to concentrate their attention on mobilization and what follows, but the implicit model of motivation underlying their concerns will affect their analyses of those problems.

This chapter will be mainly devoted to one of the most unsettled motivational issues, that regarding the recourse to deprivations or grievances as explanatory factors. But the other motivational components will also be encountered in the course of that review, which will critically examine earlier approaches, such as symbolic interactionism, value-added, and relative deprivation, as well as current perspectives, including resource mobilization, political process/contentious politics, new social movements, and social-psychological approaches, including emotions.

THE ROLE OF DEPRIVATIONS AND GRIEVANCES IN VARIOUS THEORETICAL APPROACHES

Early Collective Behaviour Approaches

As just mentioned, until the 1970s the main theorists of collective behaviour and social movements generally held that deprivations or grievances were a prime determinant in generating such phenomena. Indeed, until then the whole history of theory development in this field manifested a trend toward a gradually increasing emphasis being placed on the role of some forms of deprivation in collective behaviour.

In its early phases, with Gustave LeBon (1960 [1895]), for instance, "crowd psychology" paid no attention to real deprivations or discontent, as the masses were seen as simply acting on the basis of irrational impulses and capricious feelings spreading through suggestion. LeBon characterized the sentiments of crowds as impulsive, irritable, suggestible, and credulous, and crowds "as incapable of willing as of thinking for any length of time" (38). While much subsequent work was tainted by LeBon's misconceptions, many analysts soon distanced themselves from his views.

Indeed, although influenced by LeBon, the early American theorists in the field, identified as that of collective behaviour, generally rejected his motivational biases, in particular his assumption of irrationality (Turner and Killan 1987, 5). Herbert Blumer, for instance, argued that objective conditions of "disturbance in the usual forms of living or routines of life" produced subjective feelings of "discomfort, frustration, insecurity" and led first to personal unrest, possibly followed by social unrest. Rooted in symbolic interactionism, Blumer's work, however, placed the emphasis not on motivation but rather on the social interaction processes through which collective behaviour, including social unrest, developed and spread through circular reaction (Blumer 1955, citation from 171).

More elaborate developments of this collective behavior approach soon followed, in particular in the sophisticated work of Ralph Turner and Lewis Killian, through the three editions of their *Collective Behaviour*, all focused on the emergence of new norms as the central process accounting for the development of collective behaviour. In the first edition (1957, chap. 2), one finds, as in Blumer, only vague motivational notions of changes and inadequacies in social organization, in normative integration, and in communications. In its discussion of elementary forms of collective behaviour, the second edition (1972, especially chap. 4) similarly referred to the impact of unanticipated events, unstructured situations, structured disruptions, or value conflicts as the four types of disturbing conditions. The discussion of factors in the emergence of social movements presented in that edition (chap. 13), and even more so in the third edition (1987, chaps. 13 and 14), placed an increasing emphasis on an important motivating component emerging from objectively strained circumstances, that is, the ensuing possible development of a sense of injustice, accompanied by feelings of indignation. Movements were said to be "inconceivable apart from a vital sense that some established practice or mode of thought [was] wrong and ought to be replaced," with the common element being "the conviction that existing conditions [were] unjust." The authors also analyzed in detail the factors leading to collective redefinitions of these objective conditions as felt grievances or injustices and the conditions leading these feelings to collective action. In particular, hope in the possibility of change "opens the gates to movement formation" (1987, 242, 246). Finally, in that edition of the book, one finds a first, but brief, discussion of the Olsonian problem and of the motivating role of selective incentives (1987, 330–4, 350–1).[2]

An important departure from those traditional social-psychological approaches, with greater stress on structural factors, occurred with the 1963 publication of Neil Smelser's path-breaking *Theory of Collective Behavior*, partly anchored in Parsonian theory for its many typological schemes. But its main innovation lay elsewhere, in the development of an analytical paradigm – the value-added model – that placed equal theoretical emphasis on a main motivational component, structural strains,[3] and on five other determinants. Smelser distinguished four types of strains, that is, ambiguities, actual or potential deprivations, norm conflicts, and value discrepancies. The other five determinants were either social-psychological but mostly structural. They were structural conduciveness, generalized beliefs, precipitating factors, mobilization of participants for action, and social control. To be sure, these determinants need not develop in that sequence, contrary to Smelser's claim (14). But all were rightly said to be necessary for collective behaviour to emerge and some of them, including strains, could be constant, as long as modifications occurred in at least one of the others.[4] A detailed analysis of the origins of strains, presumed to be located in one form or another of social disorganization, was elaborated. At the same time, the controversial notions of generalized belief and of short-circuiting processes were developed at length. While early critics seized on the shortcomings in these components (e.g., Currie and Skolnick 1970; Tilly 1973, 1975), they usually disregarded, except for Oberschall (1973), what was Smelser's major contribution, the presentation of a multidimensional, interactive, analytical model of six determinants, in which alternative notions of strains or beliefs could be easily substituted and in which neglected components of motivation, such as incentives,[5] could be introduced.[6] More recently, Crossley (2002) presented a long-awaited balanced view of Smelser's contribution; while rejecting the notion that short-circuiting processes prevail in the elaboration of generalized beliefs, Crossley nevertheless endorsed the overall value-added model.

A perspective attributing to deprivation an even greater role – indeed making it the all-important determinant – was taken later on by a group of political scientists who elaborated the relative deprivation approach (Davies 1962; Gurr 1968, 1970; Feierabend, Feierabend, and Nesvold 1969). Not only was deprivation now becoming the central focus of attention, but only a special type of deprivation – relative deprivation – was being considered. Again, to be sure, at least in Ted Gurr's work, the models developed contained other factors, some structural, such as the coercive potential of opponents, the degree of institutionalization of the intermediate structure, facilitation factors for the insurgents, and the legitimacy of the regime. But these were far from being considered as equally important as relative deprivation. The latter was considered to be "the basic precondition for civil strife of any kind," and other factors were only "mediating" or "intervening" variables that simply depressed or intensified "the fundamental relationship between deprivation and strife" (Gurr 1968, 1104–5; see also Gurr 1970, chaps. 1 and 10). By placing such an emphasis on deprivation, Davies, Gurr, and Feierabend, Feierabend, and Nesvold were leaving themselves open to serious criticisms.[7] And indeed the validity of some of these criticisms was recognized by Gurr, as his subsequent models reveal (Gurr and Duvall 1973; Gurr 1993a). The narrow notion of relative deprivation was dropped, and in the new model (1993a) it was replaced by objective disadvantages and the ensuing subjective grievances. In addition, in that theory analytical components such as mobilization and opportunities, explicitly borrowed from the resource mobilization perspective, were introduced, although barely developed. Deprivations and grievances continued to be the factors to which the greatest attention was paid.[8]

An important issue involved in the approaches reviewed so far is the relevance of the distinction between objective deprivations and felt grievances, rooted in outrage and moral indignation. Smelser, for instance, stressed the first notion, while Turner and Killian insisted that the important factor was the second. Actually, in much research the distinction is not that clearcut. The notion of objective deprivations is practically always accompanied by an implicit, when not explicit, idea that such deprivations are directly transformed into felt discontents, while the proponents of social-psychological approaches generally insist that such a translation need not automatically take place. The latter position is justified. The processes involved in such a translation, as in framing processes, must indeed be part of a fully developed social psychology of social movements, as will be seen below.[9]

The Resource Mobilization Approach

Criticisms against the above approaches came with a complete reversal of perspectives on motivational issues. This took place during the 1970s with the development of new structural approaches, the resource mobilization and the political process theories, which remain the popular perspectives.[10] The critics lumped together indiscriminately, without distinctions, all the approaches reviewed above, referring to them as the "classical model" (McCarthy and Zald 1973), "breakdown theories" (Tilly, Tilly, and Tilly 1975), or the "Durkheim formulation" (Tilly 1978). While some versions of the so-called breakdown theories, such as LeBon's approach or the mass society approach (Kornhauser 1959), stressing the effects of rootlessness and social isolation, were justly criticized and empirically unsupported,[11] the overall rejection of breakdown and disintegration has since become increasingly questioned (e.g., Useem 1985, 1998; Piven and Cloward 1992; Snow et al. 1998). In particular, disorganization can itself be one of the sources of grievances (Useem 1985, 677; Piven and Cloward 1979; Snow et al. 1998). Above all, the rejection of all deprivation claims was not justified, as argued in this chapter.

As if there were nowhere else to go from the early narrow position of relative deprivation theorists but to another extreme, the writers who developed the new perspectives generally held, first, that collective and/or selective incentives were the important motivating factors, not the deprivations or the grievances of participants. The latter were considered to be secondary or of no relevance, either because they were assumed to be constant and ubiquitous or, at any rate, because they were claimed to be unsupported by the evidence. Instead it was argued that the amount and types of resources available, their mobilization, the organization and the solidarity of the groups involved, the presence of opportunities, and the repression or facilitation encountered were the important determinants of collective action.

But while some of these authors held qualified positions (e.g., Oberschall), others (e.g., McCarthy and Zald, Tilly) originally left little or no place for deprivation. Anthony Oberschall (1973) held the most balanced views, although at first these views were not well integrated into his general perspective. He discussed at some length (chap. 2) the role of various forms of discontent and rightly argued that the role of social and institutional structures should prevent us from expecting "simple relationships of cause and effect between the magnitudes and extent of discontents and grievances" and the outbreak of collective action (64). He failed, however, to make then a clear distinction between the emergence of such action and participation in it, even though this was implicitly taken up later on (chap. 5). As will be argued below, grievances bear a more direct relationship to the second dimension, participation. His best contribution in that book was focused on mobilization, but his analyses of it started with an explicit assumption that grievances were present to begin with. In subsequent papers, however, grievances took the back seat,

as he asserted that "the central concern ... becomes mobilization, organization, and collective action" (1978a, 305) or as he
stressed only collective and selective incentives and expectancy
of success as motivational components (1980).

In subsequent writings, Oberschall's position became better
articulated and more balanced. He maintained that to explain
the emergence of social movements, four necessary (although not
sufficient) sets of factors had to be taken into account, stressing
the changes occurring in each of them. The first one directly covered discontents and grievances, as in his earlier writings, while
the other three dealt with, first, beliefs and ideologies, and their
framing; second, mobilization, or the capacity to act collectively;
and third, political opportunities (Oberschall 1993, 1996). In his
analysis of the emergence of the American women's movement,
for instance, he did pay attention to changes or the lack thereof
in all four sets of factors (1993).

John McCarthy and Mayer Zald, the main proponents of the
resource mobilization perspective, were for long far from being
equally favourable to deprivation arguments. They originally
characterized the professional social movements, claimed to be
the modern form taken by movements, as ones depending mainly
on professional organizers and having practically no membership base and therefore as ones for which members' grievances
were irrelevant. In so doing, they were completely at odds with
the view that without widespread shared grievances in a collectivity, "leaders cannot create a substantial following or a social
movement" (Oberschall 1973, 158), that if the rest of the population was not already aggrieved, elite aspirations would not
alone lead to widespread contentious action (Horowitz 1985).
For McCarthy and Zald (1973, 17, 20), grievances models were
relevant only for some – not all – movements of earlier periods.
Subsequently they wrote that they "want(ed) to move from a
strong assumption about the centrality of deprivation and grievances to a weak one," which made these factors only secondary components in the generation of social movements (1977,
1215). They added that according to the resource mobilization
perspective, "social movements may or may not be based upon
the grievances of the presumed beneficiaries" (1216) and that

at any rate one could assume "that the costs and rewards of involvement" – that is, selective incentives – "can account for individual participation" (1226). Such views are neither theoretically sound nor empirically supported.[12]

A general statement presented about ten years later (jointly with McAdam) barely showed any modification of their position (McAdam, McCarthy, and Zald 1988). While properly introducing a distinction between movement *emergence* and individual *participation*, they rejected, even in the case of participation, practically all micro-individual accounts of activism covering internal motives. These included various psychological accounts, in particular relative deprivation, but also "attitudinal correlates," which were not granted much impact. The only other type of grievances whose relevance was accepted was Edward Walsh's (1981) suddenly imposed grievances, but with reservations, since those grievances were said to rest on special sets of circumstances. Instead, to explain recruitment, one had again to turn to selective incentives, but above all to microstructural accounts, such as social networks and organizational memberships. In short, they wrote, the new approaches had led "to growing dissatisfaction with the individual accounts of activism" and "people don't participate in movements so much because they are psychologically and attitudinally compelled to, but because their structural location ... makes it easier for them to do so" (707). In an emerging synthesis presented subsequently by the same authors, more attention was paid to cultural factors, especially framing processes, but with no attention to grievances, except for a very brief mention within the section on framing (McAdam, McCarthy, and Zald 1996).[13]

It was only later that in two overlapping papers McCarthy and Zald, in response to criticisms and to empirical research, presented amending efforts. They admitted that in their early model attention to the supply side had prevailed over consideration of the demand side. With regard to the latter, they wrote that their approach "had downplayed the role of grievances in generating movements" and that "any complete account of movements must take into account how grievances and life conditions enter into mobilization" (Zald and McCarthy 2002, 161). In

the second paper, they wrote that on an empirical basis grievances did matter and that the question was when and how they
did (McCarthy and Zald 2002, 557). They recognized, however,
that a more integrated view of cultural dimensions within their
theory was still lacking. Indeed, as is often noted, their framework simply lacked a social psychology of social movements.[14]

The Political Process and Contentious Politics Approaches

One is hard put, however, to find such qualified statements
among the main proponents of the other structural perspective,
the *political process* approach, more recently recast as the *contentious politics* approach, currently the dominant paradigm in
the study of non-routine collective action. If anything, that perspective has over time gradually moved further away from any
consideration of motivational concerns. This increasing silence
can be observed in particular in the work of Charles Tilly, the
leading proponent of this perspective. While his general structural analyses fully deserved the recognition they have received,
the same cannot be said about his social psychology. Indeed Tilly
held negative views regarding the role of any type of deprivation. It is important to note first that the central concern in this
approach is, even more so than in the other approaches reviewed
so far, with the emergence of collective action, not with participation in it, something more likely to lead to such views.

Like so many others, Tilly of course rightly rejected the mass
society theory and older versions of the so-called breakdown
approaches, such as the idea that contentious collective action
could be the result of displaced tensions and generalized anxieties resulting from various forms of structural disruption, as
in the LeBon tradition. But he also tended to reject all other
deprivation versions. While his harshest criticisms were repeatedly directed against relative deprivation theory, his views about
any other deprivation or grievance arguments, although at
times more ambiguous, were also generally negative. His position rested on the conviction that there is no single relationship between deprivation and the emergence of collective action
– something widely accepted – and that grievances can rarely be

the triggering factor of the latter – something very questionable. With regard to the motivating role of deprivation behind individual participation, the question was largely ignored and by implication the idea appeared also to be rejected (Tilly 1978; see also Snyder and Tilly 1972; Tilly 1975; Tilly, Tilly, and Tilly 1975). And contrary to the positions of Oberschall and of McCarthy and Zald, his views never evolved, as revealed, for instance, by the latest version of the theory, the contentious politics model, co-authored with Sidney Tarrow, in which the issue of grievances is occasionally disparaged and generally ignored (Tilly and Tarrow 2007),[15] except for an admission at the very end of the book that they "had little to say about the social psychology of contention" (196), referring readers instead to Klandermans' book (1997).

With deprivation arguments so disregarded, Tilly's models (e.g., 1978) start with the notion that collective action is initiated with solidary groups making claims on behalf of their interests, these interests acting as the key motivating factor. But interests are a given, assumed to be present (1978, 200, 228) and implicitly as mostly stable, so that they cannot be triggering factors either; this argument has been challenged, since interests could in fact be emergent (Jenkins 1983, 549). But according to Tilly, the triggering factors are to be found in the structural factors that follow, that is organization, mobilization, repression, power, and above all opportunity/threat.[16] No consideration is explicitly given to the possibility that variations in internal motives might matter much in pushing actors to making such claims. Is it not possible that the extent and intensity of felt grievances, together with the strong emotions they usually generate, as opposed to simple, cold aspirations, might be important determinants of the strength of such claims making and that therefore all of this could be theoretically highly relevant?[17] Is this not particularly true in the case of exceptional economic distress among the lower classes, as argued by Piven and Cloward (1979, chap. 1) regarding the great depression of the 1930s? Or even during less serious recessions, but with very high unemployment rates, as in Quebec during the late 1950s and early 1960s (Pinard 1975)?

Now, in Tilly's work the notion of interest is not without serious ambiguities. To be sure, interests are defined very precisely
and narrowly as "the gains and losses" or "the shared advantages or disadvantages" likely to accrue to contenders as a result
of their actions (Tilly, 1978, 7, 54). These are clearly *external collective goods*. While in general the concept of interests connotes
larger and less precise notions, including *internal drives and
needs* as well as external goods,[18] these external goods are the
components generally stressed in Tilly's work. Notice that Tilly
often slipped into such wider notions, something that led him
to reintroduce grievances through the back door. Thus he occasionally used three terms together, writing about people jointly
acting on the basis of their "interests, grievances, and aspirations" or "grievances, hopes, and interests" or the like (e.g., Tilly
1978, 6, 228–34; 1981, 15; 1986, 3). Interests, the presence of
which is assumed, are even said to be imputed either from historical analysis or by paying attention "to what people say are
their grievances, aspirations, and rights" (Tilly 1978, 228). In
my view, grievances and aspirations are two important *internal*
motives underlying the pursuit of interests in the narrow sense
of the term, that is *external* collective advantages to be obtained
or disadvantages to be avoided. Moreover, as will be argued,
whether in concrete situations mainly grievances or mainly simple aspirations are involved can make much difference.

More generally, it is in Tilly's subsequent discussion of revolutions that deprivation arguments become more explicit, with
the commitment of large segments of the subject population
to the challenging groups viewed as mostly dependent on the
sudden failure of a government to meet specific crucial obligations or a rapid or unexpected increase in government demands,
or the threats thereof, for tax increases, military conscriptions,
the commandeering of land, crops, and farm animals, and the
like (Tilly 1978, 204–9). Analogous deprivation arguments can
be found in his discussion of the reactive or defensive form of
collective action (Tilly 1978, 146).[19] In short, the ambiguity
remains. Deprivations are not completely absent from some ad
hoc discussions, but they are conflated, within interests, with

external goods, and they remain absent in his general theoretical statements. They deserve to be explicitly and unambiguously introduced separately in any valid model of contentious collective action. The same goes for aspirations.

A no less serious source of ambiguity can be observed in Tilly's original discussion of *threats,* which are presented as the opposite of opportunities. Threats ought to be considered as belonging to a different level of analysis. While opportunities are objective structural conditions that could affect a person's motives (see chapter 6), objective or felt threats, as subtypes of deprivations and grievances, are components of motivation, felt directly, as potential, anticipated ones rather than past or current ones. It took a long time for political process theorists to recognize that (see Tarrow 2001, 12). Threats were no longer seen as simply "the flip side" of opportunities and had to be treated independently of one another (Steinberg 2005, 35). To this end, Goldstone and Tilly, who initiated the revision, introduced a distinction between current threats, defined as harms that are currently experienced or anticipated, and repressive threats, as harms expected if protest is undertaken and met with repression (Goldstone and Tilly 2001, 184–5). Since that revision,[20] threats have increasingly become considered as a major motivating factor among political process theorists (McAdam 2001, 2003; Kousis and Tilly 2005b; Steinberg 2005; Tilly and Tarrow 2007). Now whether all those types of harms are somewhat confusedly labelled as threats or whether, as should be more appropriately done, the experienced ones are considered to be actual deprivations or grievances and the anticipated or expected ones to be potential objective or felt threats is not the important issue. The essential point is that they all constitute different types of deprivations. In addition, threats can greatly increase the sense of grievances, as when the anticipation of increased hardships accompanies current ones.[21]

In short, Tilly's ambiguities seem to stem from a view according to which grievances, as well as all other internal motives such as aspirations and hopes, are simply underlying pillars of external interests and that a theory can start from those interests and disregard what analytically precedes them. This is highly questionable. It will make a great deal of difference, for instance, whether people are moved by serious grievances or simply by aspirations. In a discussion of the role of aspirations in chapter 4, it will be argued that contentious mobilization on the basis of aspirations shared mainly by elite members is likely to be much less frequent and intense and less likely to create impressive followings than contentious mobilization based on serious grievances shared by both leaders and rank and file constituency members.

Tilly's stances on deprivation were accepted by most proponents of the political process approach (e.g., Jenkins and Perrow 1977; Jenkins 1983).[22] Let us review only the positions of two of his more recent and closest associates, Sidney Tarrow and Doug McAdam, briefly cited previously. In his earlier work on protest in Italy, Tarrow's analysis (1989a) did place much emphasis on grievances, arguing "that people go out into the streets and protest in response to deeply felt grievances and opportunities" (13). Grievances were clearly distinguished from demands for some goods, the two being the objects of separate typologies and detailed empirical attention (chap. 5), with, in the end, "people's demands" being said to have "emerged from their everyday grievances" (138).[23]

Subsequently, however, Tarrow gradually moved to considering only the external components as motivating factors. In his major work, *Power in Movement* (1998), he wrote that people join movements on the basis of common claims against their opponents motivated by their common interests and values (6) and that deprivations cannot explain outbreaks of contention, since they are more constant than these outbreaks (71). But here again we find ambiguities. Only a few pages earlier, Tarrow had written that in the past, contentious politics "expressed people's immediate grievances directly," but that it was only since the eighteenth century that collective action involved a variety of social actors making a number of different claims around "broader and more proactive demands" (66–7). Tarrow seemed therefore to be wavering between two positions: one, that grievances are always too constant to be triggering factors of action;

and, two, that grievances are always important in the initiation of contention, but that in the past, this was not done without a consideration of demands and now, this is done without the articulation of the underlying grievances.

Moreover, his assertions are not consistent with his views on framing (chap. 7), which is said to be necessary to translate material interests into action. Indeed in that analysis, he does briefly concur in the views of Gamson, Snow, and their respective collaborators, according to which framing consists in both articulating grievances and identifying injustices, and in elaborating demands favouring group interests (see the social-psychology section below). Moreover, it was acknowledged, at least implicitly, that the effective framing of even permanent grievances contributes, when not to the very initiation of collective action, at the very least to its intensification, so that such grievances have at least an indirect impact on the scope of the action the group is engaged in. As mentioned above, in his more recent major work with Tilly (Tilly and Tarrow 2007), the issue of grievances is ignored altogether.

McAdam's positions on the role of deprivation followed a similar development. In his early work on the Black movement (1982), McAdam rejected the view that deprivation could be a factor in the emergence of movements because of their constant character, but nevertheless conceded that, although insufficient, they could be a necessary cause of social movements (11). Later on he argued that while objective deprivations might be constant, there was "enormous potential for variability in the subjective meanings people attach to their 'objective' situations," through cognitive liberation (33–5). Before the aggrieved people could act, they had to "collectively define their situations as unjust and subject to change through group action" (51). An important role was then assigned to felt grievances.

In a new introduction for the re-edition of his book, McAdam mentioned, but only very briefly, that "at a minimum people need to feel ... *aggrieved* about some aspect of their lives" and to develop "anger at the perceived injustice," these perceptions being developed through *"framing processes"* (1999, x; italics in original; see also McAdam and Snow 1997, 2–4, and Aminzade and McAdam 2001, 36). But the role of grievances is not theorized in McAdam's subsequent emerging dynamic model (1999, xv ff.). Other writings similarly showed increasing reticence regarding the role of grievances, as in McAdam's papers with McCarthy and Zald (1988, 1996), cited previously. Let me add that in a more recent paper attempting a synthesis of structural and cultural perspectives, the role of grievances was completely ignored (McAdam 2003).

Finally, in the first significant work co-authored by these three leading proponents of the approach (McAdam, Tarrow, and Tilly 2001), McAdam's new dynamic mobilization model was more fully developed, in an attempt to move beyond the existing resource mobilization and political process models, now dubbed the "classic model" and seen as too structural and static. But again, despite its substantial contributions, this contentious politics model ignored grievances altogether, except for discussions of threats, as well as for the suggestion that suddenly imposed grievances, enlarged to cover not only events but also the purposive actions of other contenders, can be one among many mechanisms.[24] This mechanism was, however, mentioned for a single process among many, that of regime defection (197–204).[25]

In conclusion, contrary to the authors reviewed earlier, Tarrow and McAdam have gradually moved to a further neglect of any deprivation arguments. Only their increased recognition of the importance of framing partly compensates for that neglect, even though their framing arguments are often made without much attention being paid to the diagnostic task of identifying the grievances involved.[26] Second, while the empirical case studies summarized in their work often mention data that reveal grievances, this is systematically under-theorized.

Third, as mentioned, if their argument is that aspirations and deprivations will always end up determining interests and need not therefore to be considered separately, this is highly questionable. The aspirations of the few, even when strong, will never have the same mobilizing impact as the serious grievances of large numbers, and this therefore cannot be ignored. Grievances and other internal motives, it is argued, are highly relevant to the ultimate concerns of the contentious politics proponents, that is, to "the dynamic processes through which new political actors, identities, and forms of action emerge, interact, coalesce and evolve during complex episodes of contention" (McAdam, Tarrow, and Tilly 2001, 38).

It can be added that in a related argument, Wimmer, Ceder-man, and Min (2009, 324) argue that in general, various types of grievances, aspirations, and external interests are all simultan-eously involved and that it becomes pointless to try to disentangle such intertwined and mutually reinforcing motives. In line with the contentious politics perspective, these authors urge us to turn instead to the dynamics moving motivated actors to contention. To be sure, some internal motives, such as socioeconomic status, and political grievances, could at times be fused together, but this is not always the case. In the area of ethnopolitical conflict in economically advanced nations, for instance, economically dominant groups could be moved mainly by political griev-ances (e.g., Catalonia in Spain), while economically subordinate groups could be mainly moved by their felt economic disadvan-tages (e.g., Galicia in the same country). Similarly, some ethnon-ational groups could be striving mainly for cultural incentives, others for political ones, and still others for both of these incen-tives, as well as for others. They could also face quite different patterns of collective costs. All these differences should affect, among other things, the forms, the frequency, and the intensity of conflict and the tactics and strategies followed. Such differ-ences ought therefore to be taken into account. Indeed, Wimmer and his colleagues do exactly that in their distinction between, on the one hand, competitive strivings within ethnically divided ruling elites leading to infighting and, on the other hand, polit-ical exclusion of ethnically distinct groups leading to rebellion.[27]

One reason for the salience of grievances among early theor-ists and their disregard among recent theorists is that while the emergence of contentious collective action has been the central theoretical concern in all approaches, the first focus, among most early theorists, was on the emergence of elementary forms of col-lective behaviour – crowd behaviour in panics, crazes, riots, and the like.[28] But it could be argued that these forms of collective action are more likely than social movements to be triggered by new or increasing deprivations; it is certainly the case for panics. At any rate, the attention focused on *individuals* as the engaged participants in passing crowds made it likely that their deprivations would be more striking, when compared to those of the more remote participants in social movements. Hence, among these early theorists the greater emphasis on the social psychology of recruitment, especially deprivation.

In addition, many of the after-1960 movements that recent authors have been interested in involved middle-class participants whose mobilization was not triggered by substantial increases in basic grievances but emerged under conditions of relatively stable grievances – indeed often under improving conditions.[29] These authors were therefore led to bypass motivation problems altogether and to search for triggering factors located largely in some structural dimensions. But one should not start by assuming that grievances are either generally stable or generally changing; that remains an empirical question. At any rate, as implied by Tarrow, even when they are constant, their scope and intensity could account for the scope and intensity of the collective action. And they could be necessary factors of emergence, although not triggering ones, as well as important motivating factors of recruitment.[30]

The New Social Movements Approach

While the above approaches were being developed in the United States, a distinct perspective, the new social movements approach, was proposed in Western Europe to account for the emerging movements of the 1960s. As Melucci put it, rather than being concerned, like their American counterparts, with the "how" of the development of collective action during that period, the European scholars stressed the "why" of such developments (1980, 212). What is important with regard to the concerns of this chapter is that this led the Europeans to be very concerned with two of the motivational dimensions underlying the emergence of collective action and people's participation in it, that is, grievances and collective incentives. This indeed was for them a central focus.

Starting from an analysis of fundamental structural changes in contemporary society, that is, the development of advanced capitalism, the passage from industrial to post-industrial society, and changes in the structure of production, their attention was focused on the ill effects of such transformations, identifying the new discontents and deprivations they created. The proponents of the approach shared the views that the breakdown of the old order[31] engendered contradictions, incompatibilities, and ruptures between different elements and levels of social structure, and led to technocratic domination not only in work relations but in all areas of social life and to the loss of personal and collective identities. The new movements constituted not collective action aimed at material incentives of an economic or political nature, something characteristic of the industrial era, but cross-class action towards collective incentives such as the removal of the above deprivations, the abolition of domination, the reestablishment of one's control in all areas of one's social life, and above all, as a central collective good, the construction of new individual and collective identities (Melucci 1980, 1989; Offe 1987; Touraine 1985).

Two aspects of this motivational perspective must be stressed. First, the deprivations created by modernizing changes were obviously seen not as constant but as new and increasing (on this, see Klandermans and Tarrow 1988, 7). Thus Melucci stressed the increasing distortions and degradations occurring in post-industrial society, and Offe considered the broadening of the negative side-effects of late capitalism and the deepening deprivations experienced in all aspects of personal and social existence (Melucci 1981; Offe 1987). This implies that increases in deprivations constituted important triggering factors for the new movements, in sharp contrast with the views of the American structuralists.

Second, however, the deprivations described by the European scholars were overly abstract and general and do not seem to be the only relevant ones involved. It is not clear that they affected virtually every member of society in all aspects of their lives, rather than mainly the groups getting mobilized. Moreover, it would seem reasonable to hypothesize that the specific

grievances articulated by, say, each of the ethnoregionalist movements of that period, be they economic or political, were key
internal motives, together, in various degrees, with the identity
problems mentioned. In addition these grievances were often of a
different kind than those underlying the student or the women's
or the ecology or the peace movements, to mention only a few
examples. The same goes for the collective incentives pursued,
being both material and symbolic, as is now largely recognized.
To be sure, Melucci, for instance, did not deny the singularity of
these movements, but he insisted on the importance of "what is
common beyond these differences and what is permanent beyond
the conjunctural variations" (1981, 183; 1988). The identification of some common grievances in all movements, however,
does not imply that those grievances always constituted the
essential motivating factors. One can recognize that those common elements coloured the general modes of collective action in
all movements, their organizations and tactics, their values, but
one can question Touraine's claim (1985) – albeit also rejected
by Melucci (1989, 80) – that there was but one basic movement,
and, more generally, the hypothesis that pervades that approach,
making the same general deprivations of postindustrial society
the determining internal motives of all new movements. Now,
of course, this implies that they were not general triggering factors either. Indeed, as argued later, the specific grievances underlying some of these movements, particularly the communal ones,
tended to be relatively constant.

Another perspective, one that is in some ways akin to this
approach and that is mainly associated with the work of Inglehart (e.g., 1990), also stresses the causal impact of broad
processes of social changes, but of a cultural rather than a
structural nature. These changes are identified as passages from
materialist to postmaterialist values. This perspective is, however, quite different from the perspectives just reviewed. For
one thing, this approach sees these changes not as negative ill
effects of post-industrialism but as resulting from the rapid economic growth and security in advanced industrial societies generating life satisfaction and allowing for a shift to higher-level

needs of self-expression, quality of life, and personal growth, which remained unmet. Second, these changes are seen as not necessarily providing the basic motivational forces for the various new movements but as dynamic, albeit secondary, forces facilitating the emergence of the new movements and the expression of their specific grievances. Indeed, Inglehart (1995) argues, for instance, that both objective environmental problems and subjective postmaterialist values account for environmental movements.

Social-Psychological and Cultural Perspectives

Reacting against the excessive emphasis on structural factors in the resource mobilization and political process perspectives, many researchers soon insisted on the necessity to complement those perspectives with a social psychology of social movements and, in particular, with constructionist perspectives. While often sympathetic to structural perspectives, the proponents of these approaches claimed that ideational and other cultural factors, dominant in early collective behaviour theories, had to be rejuvenated – once freed of "the old baggage of irrationality and social pathology" (Gamson 1992b, 54) – and brought into syntheses with these structural perspectives, since "social psychology is an indispensable component of an adequate theory of resource mobilization" (Gamson, Fireman, and Rytina 1982, 9; also Jenkins 1983; Ferree and Miller 1985; Snow et al. 1986; Mueller 1992; Snow and Oliver 1995, 590).

In this regard, some have developed general social-psychological models, while others have been concerned with more specific cultural issues, such as framing processes involved in collective action, the impact of emotional feelings in motivating participants, and the role of collective identification and solidarity in mobilization processes. Different aspects of these problems are of direct relevance to our concerns and will be examined immediately. The examination of the role of collective identities, whose impact on motivation is particularly important, will, however, be postponed until chapter 6.

THE FRAMING PERSPECTIVE

The framing perspective has become extremely popular. In line with our concerns, the first thing to mention is that in the work on framing, grievances are a central determinant. Its first proponent among collective action students was William Gamson. Drawing, among others, on Turner and Killian and on early work by McAdam, for whom, as seen above, a sense of injustice was essential in accounting for social movements, Gamson and his associates showed in their experimental research that an important condition for participation in rebellious action was the collective adoption of an *injustice frame*, simply defined as involving the belief that the actions of the authorities, if unimpeded, would result in an unjust situation for those involved (Gamson, Fireman, and Rytina 1982).

In a subsequent study, Gamson (1992a) returned to such concerns, focusing on the construction of meanings and political consciousness. Borrowing from Snow and Benford, he considered collective action frames as action-oriented sets of beliefs and meanings that inspire and legitimate social movement activities and campaigns (7). He further distinguished three components of framing, that is, injustice, involving moral indignation against those responsible for it; agency, as a consciousness of political efficacy; and identity, the definition of a "we" and an adversarial "they." His empirical investigation led him to the conclusion that the injustice component was facilitating the adoption of the other two elements and was indeed "the key to integrating all three elements of collective action frames" (114). From our perspective, however, collective identities are not, as is often assumed, motives for action themselves; they belong to a different level of analysis, although, as will be seen in chapter 6, they could be important determinants of another motive, moral obligations. Indeed collective identities constitute independent factors that could affect other motivational components as well.[32]

The framing approach was the subject of greater elaboration in the work of David Snow and his collaborators and of many of their followers, and it has become a central perspective alongside structural ones. In a first paper on the subject, one finds again grievances as an important element, not as objective conditions but as the interpretations and subjective meanings attached to them (Snow et al. 1986; Snow and Oliver 1995, 586). Framing was seen as the *signifying* work of participants and leaders of social movements. "They frame, or assign meaning to and interpret, relevant events and conditions in ways that are intended to mobilize adherents and constituents, to garner bystander support, and to demobilize antagonists." In turn, collective action frames are the products of framing activity (Snow and Benford 1988, 198; 1992). The construction of meanings is said to arise "through interactively based interpretive processes" (Snow 2004, 384). This involves three core tasks: *diagnostic* framing, the identification of a problematic situation and its redefinition as unjust or immoral[33] and the attribution of blame for it; *prognostic* framing, the suggestion of solutions[34] and the identifications of strategies, tactics, and targets; and *motivational* framing, a call to arms or rationale for engaging in corrective action (Snow and Benford 1988, 1992, 137; Benford and Snow 2000).

As we have seen, a few of the structuralists have paid some attention to framing, but it is noteworthy that in their discussions of it, grievances are only of minor concern compared to the central place they occupy in the framing perspective. I will return to the general impact of framing on motivation in chapter 6.

GENERAL SOCIAL PSYCHOLOGICAL PERSPECTIVES

While other social psychological dimensions such as collective identity, solidarity, consciousness, and affective dimensions are also considered in the work of Gamson, of Snow, and of their collaborators (e.g., Gamson 1992b; Snow and Oliver 1995), one has to turn to Bert Klandermans' *The Social Psychology of Protest* (1997) to get a fuller social psychological theory, which also constitutes an effort to integrate such a theory with the structural perspectives. Let us briefly review for the moment the parts of his contribution directly relevant to motivational dimensions.

According to Klandermans, who closely follows Gamson, the first process towards participation in a movement is the generation of a collective action frame, and the first component of such a frame involves again some feelings of injustice, as outrage regarding the authorities' treatment of a social problem (38); "felt injustice," writes Klandermans, "is at the roots of any protest" (205). Klandermans distinguishes three kinds of grievances as components of such feelings: the perception of illegitimate inequality, suddenly imposed grievances, and moral indignation about the violations of moral principles. The other framing components involve, as in Gamson, collective identities or consciousness, leading to "we" and "they" feelings, and a factor of agency, as a belief that collective action can be effective. Of course such a frame is not an objective fact to be taken for granted; it must be collectively constructed, and it must be appropriated by potential participants. All this leads to someone's adherence to a movement, as simple attitudinal support, that is, to consensus mobilization (chap. 2). The more successful the framing, the stronger the adherence developed.

While necessary, this process is, however, not sufficient. It must be followed by the translation of discontent into participation, that is by action mobilization, in which adherents are converted into actual contributors. This involves, in particular, reaching adherents and overcoming the dilemma of participating in the pursuit of a collective good by the appropriate play of collective and selective incentives, benefits and costs of participation (chap. 3). The discussion of some of these processes is postponed to subsequent sections. In more recent papers (Klandermans 2004; Van Stekelenburg and Klandermans 2007, especially 179ff.; Klandermans, Van der Toorn, and Van Stekelenburg 2008), the motivation model is modified, but the original instrumental motives (Klandermans 1984), especially grievances, are kept, now combined with greater insistence on identity motives and the introduction of emotional and ideological motives, the ideological ones referring to desires to express one's views, "to gain dignity and moral integrity" (2007, 183).

The essential point of this review of framing and other social-psychological perspectives is that they all consider felt grievances as very critical components for an adequate analysis of contentious collective action. In this regard the relative silence of proponents of mobilization and process perspectives remains difficult to understand, except as undue generalizations of their reactions to the shortcomings of early approaches and their stress on irrational and pathological responses to discontents.

GRIEVANCES AND EMOTIONS

Emotions were deemed very important in traditional collective behaviour approaches, and for good reasons. Their role is much more important in contentious action than in routine institutionalized action. In the former the intensity of concerns prevailing among participants is likely to be stronger, and the type of concrete actions engaged in are more likely to take people outside ordinary routines of social life (e.g., Snow and Oliver 1995; Calhoun 2001). The silence of structural theorists in this regard was therefore paradoxical, ultimately leading to severe criticisms. In addition, criticisms were also leveled at writers who had devoted much effort to integrating cultural dimensions within structural theories, especially through the framing perspective. The critics stressed their overemphasis on cognitive components and processes and their disregard of affective, emotional, dimensions.[35] A focus on emotions, it was argued, would provide much insight into various social movement processes and in particular into people's motivations for participating in them (Gould 2004). Given my central focus on motivation in this work, the problem of emotions ought to be given serious consideration.

But a qualification can first be entered. The analysts who have traditionally asserted that felt, or intensely felt, grievances, not just cognitively assessed deprivations, ought to be considered acknowledged at least implicitly the presence of emotional sentiments, although without specifying the emotions involved. Feeling aggrieved is after all a sentiment at the core of the emotional dimension.[36] This is not to say that more explicit recognition of emotions, and especially of the various types of them, is not warranted; it is.

Serious attention to emotions started to develop mainly during the 1990s, often among the authors discussed in the last two sections. But one already finds attention paid to emotions before that. In a paper of the early 1980s, Lofland, in an effort "to bring emotions back into the study of collective behaviour," argued that there were "three fundamental emotions" – fear, hostility, and joy – and used them as basic classifying dimensions of three forms of collective behaviour and their many subtypes (e.g., panics, hostile crowds, and crazes).This work, however, presented largely descriptive typologies and failed to pay serious attention to other motives, in particular to underlying grievances (Lofland 1985, chaps. 1 and 2, reproducing earlier papers; citations from 39, 69). Let us turn to subsequent writings, which were more elaborate.

While in their early work on framing, Gamson, Fireman, and Rytina (1982) had been more concerned with the cognitive judgments concerning the injustices created, Gamson (1992a, 7, 31–3, 185) was subsequently clearly calling attention to the emotions that could also be involved. Borrowing from psychologists the notion of "hot cognition – one that is laden with emotion," he referred to the sentiments of "moral indignation" and "righteous anger" likely to accompany situations involving injustices,[37] particularly when the persons or groups responsible for them were concretely identified; resignation was otherwise likely to prevail. Klandermans (1997, 17, 38; see also 2004) soon followed Gamson's views, writing about the "moral indignation," the "anger and moral outrage" derived from grievances, defining indeed feelings of injustice as outrage about the authorities' treatment of problems. Similarly the role of emotions became central in Taylor's many analyses of the feminist movement, with her insistence that emotions were a no less important "motivating" factor than material interests. She even linked different emotions to different motivational components: to deprivations first, such as power and status inequalities, with the emotion of anger as a response to gender injustice but also to social selective incentives, based on "the joy of participation, the love and friendship of other women, pride at having maintained their feminist convictions" (Taylor 1995, 224, 228; also 1989, and her 2010 paper reviewing her work in this regard).

But the authors most closely associated with criticisms of previous approaches and the revival of the study of emotions in social movements were Jasper and his collaborators (Jasper 1997, 1998, 2006; Goodwin, Jasper, and Polletta 2000, 2004). While rejecting the claim that emotions, pervading all social action, were irrational – an argument now generally accepted – Jasper argued that emotions do not simply accompany our desires and satisfactions but that "they constitute them, permeating our ideas, identities, and interests" (1998, 399). Not mere bodily sensations, but socially constructed, emotions were tied to both cognitive meanings and to moral values, with emotions, cognitions, and morality fused together, as core cultural components. At another level, but not fully integrated with these components nor with his basic dimensions of protest, Jasper introduced the notions of *threats* and *blame,* said to constitute "two crucial building blocks of protest" (1997, 108, 127).

With regard to the emotions relevant to protest – long detailed lists of which are presented – Jasper made an important distinction between those that are more permanent and primarily affective, such as attachments, solidarities, and loyalties, and those that are primarily reactive responses to events and information, such as anger and indignation, as well as fears of impending dangers.[38] The latter ones will retain our attention in this section. He also opposed action-oriented emotions, such as the last ones just mentioned, and withdrawal-oriented ones, such as resignation or cynicism. This distinction, also found in Klandermans, Van der Toorn, and Van Stekelenburg (2008), is significant in that it calls attention to the fact that there are both mobilizing and demobilizing emotions. In addition, emotions preceding participation in movements were distinguished from those that are developed through participation in them. Finally, Jasper argued that emotions could greatly enrich various causal mechanisms, such as moral shocks, attribution of blame, frame alignment, injustice frames, and collective identity (Jasper 1998; also Goodwin, Jasper, and Polletta 2001).

These writings on emotions have had quite an impact, even among authors from divergent perspectives. Aminzade and McAdam considered the "silence" of the social movement literature on emotions as an "especially notable" one and wrote that the mobilization of emotions was an "exceedingly important component of any significant instance of collective action" (2001, 14). Tarrow shared this view, stating that emotions are a "key factor" that "no sensible social movement scholar would

exclude" (2001, 4, 8–9; also 1998, 111–12), and Klandermans considered emotions as a central "motive" to participate
(Klandermans 2004; see also Van Stekelenburg and Klandermans 2007; Klandermans, Van der Toorn, and Van Stekelenburg
2008). Similar reactions came from Benford (1997).

But while Jasper and his collaborators criticized not only
structural theorists but also many social psychological theorists for ignoring or leaving implicit the role of emotions in their
analyses of protest, the first group could in turn be taken to task
for failing to clearly integrate emotions with deprivations, grievances, and other motivational factors. For one thing, the concepts of deprivation and grievance are largely absent from their
theory.[39] To be sure the concept of threat is apparently meant to
partly replace them, although in Jasper's 1998 paper, threats are
examined in conjunction with only one of many causal mechanisms – blame attribution. The reasons for substituting threats
for those other concepts are never discussed.[40] But the concept
of threat, when so largely generalized, is likely to create ambiguities.[41] First, the notion of threats, as general definitions of
the term indicate, should be restricted to anticipated, impending
future deprivations or grievances.[42]

More importantly, the disregard of the double notions of
objective deprivations and felt grievances and the fact that the
multiple lists of threats presented are generally objective external
situations and dangers, with infrequent references to a sense of
threats (see for instance the lists presented in Jasper 1997, table
5.2, and 1998, table 3) leave, with regard to internal motives, the
main subjective explanatory weight to emotions.[43] In the end,
emotions appear to be the key, if not the sole, motivating factor
of protest, at the expense of felt grievances and their discontents,
which should be presumed to precede emotions.[44] No independent discussion of the specific role of deprivations or grievances
(or threats, for that matter) in the generation of emotions ever
follows, in contrast to what one finds, for instance, in Gamson
(1992a), Taylor (1995, 2010), Van Zomeren et al. (2004), and
Klandermans, Van der Toorn, and Van Stekelenburg (2008). To
be sure, there are occasional mentions that behind specific emotions there are objective deprivations, such as disadvantageous

conditions or specific problems (see, for instance, Jasper 1998; Goodwin, Jasper, and Polletta 2001), but the role of felt grievances is ignored and the role of deprivations is seen first and foremost through their emotional expressions.

To clarify these matters, one must go beyond detailed lists of emotions or assertions that emotions are important and integrate them with other motivational dimensions, as will be done in the model to be presented.[45] Concerning the latter, a first claim is not only that cognitive and emotional dimensions must be considered separately but that observed deprivations and felt grievances, as well as the emotions they generate, must be kept analytically distinct. This allows, for instance, the development of the following propositions. First, the presence and strength of emerging (reactive) emotions are in large measure first dependent on the severity of the objective deprivations assessed and, especially, of the felt grievances generated. Of course, strong emotions once generated could in turn strengthen one's sense of grievances. This proposition would appear obvious – and it is supported in the research of Van Zomeren et al. (2004) and Klandermans, Van der Toorn, and Van Stekelenburg. (2008). The severity of the felt grievances and the strength of the emerging emotions could jointly be used as a measure of the strength of what will be labelled grievances/emotions internal motives. While felt grievances and emotions are closely akin to one another, they could vary somewhat independently. One could, for instance, feel that a condition is unjust or illegitimate but develop only little emotion about it. When both are, however, present, the spur to action is likely to be very strong. Conversely strong emotions could function as accelerators and amplifiers of weaker grievances (Van Stekelenburg and Klandermans 2007, 183; Klandermans, Van der Toorn, and Van Stekelenburg 2008). Finally grievances/emotions motives – if of course the emotions are action-oriented (e.g., anger) – should be considered as significant internal motives of attitudinal support and action participation.[46]

Other internal motives, such as moral obligations, as well as external incentives and expectancy of success, are also likely to be accompanied, indeed amplified, by their own related emotions (Klandermans, Van der Toorn, and Van Stekelenburg 2008, 995). These emotions include pride regarding altruistic contributions, joy from anticipated gains, and hope or enthusiasm regarding expected success. In each case these cognitive and affectual dimensions should be kept analytically distinct, with their respective impact considered. Much of this is already found in the literature reviewed in this section; this will be considered in subsequent discussions of these other motivational components.

Finally, as is implicit in the above discussions, the strength of the emotions involved can be the object of large variations, according to the type of participants and the types of movements considered, to mention but a few distinctions. Generally, writers on emotions tend to consider them as always quite strong. But this is obviously not the case. For instance, among leaders and highly involved militants – who were often the main subjects in emotion studies – emotions are likely to be much more intense and effective, but larger numbers of followers with minimal participation, as well as simple adherents and bystanding publics, could manifest relatively weaker emotions. Anger, outrage, or moral indignation might be good descriptions for the emotions observed among of members of the first group, but mild irritation or simple annoyance might often better describe the emotions of many of those belonging to the second group. Similarly, as another example, expressions of rage manifested in urban riots could vary in forms, if not in intensity, when compared to the indignation expressed in middle-class movements (Aminzade and McAdam 2001, 27, 31).

CONCLUDING REMARKS

In an effort to start moving beyond the controversies surrounding the role of deprivations and grievances in contentious collective action, it was claimed, first, that even if one were to grant primacy to mobilization processes and what follows, one would still need an appropriate motivation model, something currently missing in structural approaches. Second, in trying to identify the motivating factors underlying people's contributions to such action, it was hypothesized that one internal motive, covering objective deprivations, felt grievances, and emotions played a central role. To be sure, two other types of internal motives, aspirations and moral obligations, must also be taken into account. But the discussion of these two components is postponed until chapter 4.

Ultimately, the decision as to which of the claims regarding the effects of deprivations and grievances reviewed in this chapter are more valid must depend on empirical evidence. And there is a lot of such evidence, although it is occasionally inconsistent. Given the intensity of the controversies in this regard, it is rather amazing to realize that so little has been done in terms of comprehensive reviews of past empirical work and in terms of trying to account for the real or apparent inconsistencies observed. All too often, an author's claims are accompanied by selective, short, and uncritical summaries of a few studies supporting the author's position. In the next chapter, a discussion of empirical controversies about the role of grievances will first be examined, to be followed by an extensive review of the evidence, with efforts to account for inconsistent results, whenever present. Chapter 4 will press further the more fundamental methodological problems encountered in that research.

Controversies and Empirical Evidence regarding the Role of Grievances

Fundamental paradigmatic considerations clearly lie behind the rejection of the role of grievances among proponents of the resource mobilization and political process/contentious politics approaches, at least in some of the early writings. But these positions also rest, singly or jointly, on questionable considerations. First, some authors question the direction of causality generally assumed between grievances and mobilization. Second, as reported above, those who rejected deprivation hypotheses often explicitly argued that deprivations were constant and ubiquitous and that therefore they could not account for the locations and for changing levels of collective action. But regardless of the validity of that last proposition, the agnostics regularly claimed that the available evidence failed to support deprivation hypotheses or showed that at best grievances turned out to be unimportant, secondary determinants. Let us examine these claims.

THE DIRECTION OF CAUSALITY BETWEEN GRIEVANCES AND MOBILIZATION

It is at times argued that felt grievances are the result of mobilization, not the other way around (Jenkins 1981; Nagel and Olzak 1982). Thus, in a discussion of ethnic conflict, Nagel and Olzak wrote that they believed "that claims of injustice and inequality follow from ethnic mobilization rather than cause it" (136n). It can be mentioned that similar claims could be made for models in which interest replaces deprivation as motive for action. To be sure, without some form of longitudinal studies, which clearly establish the time order of these variables, it is often difficult to establish which one came first (Klandermans 1997, 218ff.), although other arguments have been used to establish the precedence of grievances (see Biggs 2006 and Pinard and Hamilton 1987).

At any rate no one would deny that in the construction and articulation of a developed injustice frame and its accompanying emotions, as was seen, the contributions of mobilizing agents are likely to be important. Moreover, through time, with increased involvement, the sense of grievances and the emotions of already mobilized participants may become stronger, not to mention the development of new grievances resulting from the coercive actions of their opponents. It is also possible for collective action originally based on the aspirations of some elite groups to become intensified if participants subsequently develop feelings that those aspirations have been unduly blocked (Bélanger and Pinard 1991).

But the framing process is an interactive one involving both leaders and prospective adherents, and these adherents do not always enter the process empty-handed. Depending in particular on the seriousness of the adverse objective situations encountered, the strength of the indignation, and the sense of injustice developed, as well as the adherents' strong personality, their degree of critical sophistication, their social and political involvement, and that of their social networks, it is not impossible for varying proportions of them to spontaneously develop feelings of injustice well before efforts to mobilize them are made.[1] This is indeed necessarily true for the initiators of a movement, its first self-recruited leaders, unless one claims they are entirely moved by aspirations for some selective incentives of a political, status, or other nature. Indeed, for the adherents, the success of any mobilizing efforts will largely depend on their pre-existing suffering resulting from adverse conditions. Finally, the greater the sense of grievances and emotions developed by participants through these processes, the greater their subsequent likelihood and degree of action mobilization.

THE CONSTANCY AND UBIQUITY OF GRIEVANCES

The argument that grievances were constant over time and ubiquitous over entire populations investigated was made early on
by Jenkins and Perrow, who wrote that it was "more fruitful
to assume that grievances are relatively constant and pervasive" and that they could account for neither the emergence of
collective protest nor participation in it (1977, 266, 250; also
Jenkins 1981, 97). The constancy argument was also made by
Oberschall in an early paper (1978a, 298), and McCarthy and
Zald wrote that "there are always grievances at large among
the citizenry" (1973, 22; also 1977, 1215). As seen before and
in somewhat more qualified ways, Tarrow wrote that the deprivations people suffer "are far more enduring than the movements they support" and that what varies widely through time
and place are opportunities, constraints, and threats (1998, 71),
and McAdam argued that objective deprivations were constant,
although their subjective meanings could vary widely (1982, 11,
33–5). In short, deprivations are said first to be so ubiquitous
that no variations across individuals, groups, or societies can be
found and that therefore such deprivations cannot explain variations in levels of mobilization. Second, deprivations are said to
be so constant through time that they cannot explain why the
emergence of protest occurs during certain periods and not during others.

That such overall arguments could have been made is simply
amazing. To be sure it is empirically obvious that there are deprivations that are largely constant, at least during periods preceding the occurrence of movements. This is the case, for instance,
for the severe disadvantages of people living at poverty or near
poverty levels or, less seriously, for members of the lower classes.
The same holds for various levels of lasting deprivations within
communal groups – gender, ethnic, racial, regional, or religious
groups – occupying subordinate positions along one or many
socio-political dimensions. Of course, to the extent that deprivations are constant, they could not be the triggering, discrimina-
tory factor for the emergence of protest, nor the decisive factor

leading one to participate. In such cases, other motivational or structural factors must be considered.[2] Conversely, how could one deny that within most groups or societies, or subgroups within them, there are large variations in the scope and intensity of experienced disadvantages? Or that, through time, many forms of deprivations can vary, possibly to a large extent, such as in the good and bad phases of economic cycles or political stages, or as consequences of changing structural arrangements of one kind or another? Or that some groups could face new emerging threats or suddenly imposed grievances resulting from the actions of authorities or other challengers or from various exceptional events?

And indeed, the constancy claims were rejected by many, as well as challenged in much research. Let me mention for the moment only that some commentators explicitly rebuffed those arguments. Turner and Killian called those assertions "extreme" and "as inadequate as the oversimplified grass-roots explanation" in accounting for the emergence of movements (1972, 251). Such claims, they wrote, outstrip the available evidence (1987, 235). While recognizing that the emergence of some movements (e.g., the ecology and women's movements) were mainly answers to long-standing grievances, not growing ones, Turner wrote that the constancy assertions are contradicted by many instances of movements that arose directly as responses to developing grievances, as for instance the America First movement and the movement for American withdrawal from Vietnam (1981, 16–18). Piven and Cloward similarly rejected the constancy arguments on the basis, among other things, that political process theorists, in their own empirical work, often showed that changing levels of grievances (e.g., among food rioters, land squatters, and machine breakers) accounted for the occurrence of protest. Following Kerbo's distinctions and arguments (1982), Piven and Cloward concluded that growing deprivations could be particularly relevant for the emergence of "movements of crisis," as opposed to "movements of affluence," in which this would not be a crucial factor (1992, 305–8). Finally, in a study of the anti-busing movement, the results led Useem (1980) to explicitly reject the argument that deprivations, because ubiquitous, were irrelevant to explaining movement participation.[3]

In addition to explicit discussions of the constancy arguments, it will be shown below that there is much evidence regarding the positive impact of grievances regarding both the occurrence of contentious protest and participation in it. But some theoretical fallacies surrounding the role of grievances, constant or not, should be dispelled immediately. As is the case in most perspectives, it is correctly assumed that multidimensional, multiplicative models are needed to properly account for collective protest. Now deprivations and grievances are one of the necessary components of such models. Where confusions appear is in the often implicit view that those components cannot be necessary[4] if they are constant or ubiquitous.[5] It must be realized that even under those conditions, grievances are still necessary, and their levels will have effects, although logically they cannot then be the *triggering* factors of protest. As long as at least one component of the model proposed is changing, this is sufficient to explain changes in levels of protest or of participation in it. This will be examined in greater detail later.

THE EVIDENCE REGARDING THE IMPACT OF GRIEVANCES

In the examination of the evidence, the distinction between the emergence of collective action and participation in it will again turn out to be very important. While all theorists, as mentioned before, have been clearly concerned with the emergence problem, this concern was more central among relative deprivation and resource mobilization/political process theorists, while the participation problem was more central among those belonging to other perspectives. Among researchers, however, the emphasis varied. Those following one of the early approaches have overwhelmingly been concerned with the individual participation problem. They have typically considered a single instance of collective behavior, trying to answer indirectly the emergence problem by an empirical investigation of the recruitment of participants. Conversely, researchers following relative deprivation and structural theories started from series of protest episodes, focusing more closely on the development of such events.

What does the evidence concerning the effects of grievances in such events indicate? One would have expected it to settle the issue, but unfortunately it did so only partly. Our critical examination of the evidence will first consider individual participation studies, in which the results are largely positive. This will be followed by a consideration of emergence studies, in which results appear inconsistent. Longitudinal studies, aiming to explain when collective protest occurred, and cross-sectional ecological studies, aiming to explain where it occurred, will be examined successively. In the next chapter, I will then try to untangle the reasons behind the inconsistent findings observed, something, it will be argued, that largely resulted from data and measurement problems and from problems of analytical designs.

Individual Participation Studies

The list of participation studies with positive results is very long indeed. Referring exclusively to quantitative survey research for the moment, which goes as far back as the 1930s, it is possible, even without claiming to be exhaustive, to cite a very large number of studies establishing positive and mostly strong relationships between deprivation and participation in, or attitudinal support for, contentious collective action (not to mention clear indications that without widespread deprivations, many movements would not have developed very far or would not have experienced the success they did.)

Thus, for instance, from the early days of survey research, positive relationships between deprivations and grievances such as unemployment, job insecurities, other socioeconomic or political deprivations, and threats, and some forms of participation in, or support for, contentious collective action were established in a large number of studies, too numerous to be reviewed in detail (Hall 1934; Centers 1949, chaps. 10–11; Leggett 1964; Hamilton 1967, chap. 9; Morrison and Steeves 1967; Zeitlin 1967, chap. 2; Aiken, Ferman, and Sheppard 1968, chap. 6; Pinard, Kirk, and Von Eschen 1969; Von Eschen, Kirk, and Pinard 1969;

Paige 1971; Pettigrew and Riley 1971; Irvine 1972; Cuneo and Curtis 1974; Wood 1974, chap. 12; Pinard 1975, chap. 6; Pinard and Hamilton 1977, 1978; Low-Beer 1978, chap. 6; Isaac, Mutran, and Stryker 1980, the hypothesis being supported with the data for Blacks; Skogstad 1980; Walsh 1981; Gamson, Fireman, and Rytina 1982; LeCavalier 1983; Muller and Jukam 1983; Opp 1988; Muller, Dietz, and Finkel 1991; Finkel and Muller 1998; Smith and Ortiz 2002; Van Zomeren et al. 2004; Klandermans, Van der Toorn, and Van Stekelenburg. 2008; Taylor et al 2009).[6]

More specifically, ethnic, racial, and other kinds of deprivations, either relative or absolute, have repeatedly been found to be related to participation in, and support for, ethnic and racial collective action (Matthews and Prothro 1966, chap. 14; Ransford 1968; Pinard, Kirk, and Von Eschen 1969; Sears and McConahay 1970; Pinard and Hamilton 1978; Useem 1980; Boldt 1981; Guimond and Dubé-Simard 1983; Pinard and Hamilton, 1986; Bélanger and Pinard 1991; Nadeau and Fleury 1995; Pinard 1997b; Roefs, Klandermans, and Olivier 1998; Mendelsohn 2003; Piroth 2004; Biggs 2006). These lists of studies could be much longer if those based solely on observational and/or historical data were also cited (e.g., Lipset 1950; Rudé 1964; Piven and Cloward 1979).[7]

It must be stressed, however, that often in these same studies *poverty* or *low socio-economic position* were found to impede participation in social movements, at least in their early phases, because too many additional conditions were missing, such as the absence of expectancy of success or political efficacy, lack of power and other resources, lack of organization, and the presence of strong social control (see the review of many studies in Pinard 1975, chap. 8; see also, for instance, Zeitlin 1967, 63ff.; Marx 1967, 62ff; Caplan 1970; Jenkins 1982). But, the poor tended to be the most supportive once involved or if experiencing additional deprivations, such as unemployment (Pinard, Kirk, and Von Eschen 1969; Pinard 1975, 148). They were also said to be prone to sudden and short-lived unorganized flare-ups under new deprivations (Oberschall 1973, chap. 4; Piven and

Cloward 1979). Poverty also appeared to be exerting restraining effects in race riots, as will be discussed below.

This is not to deny the existence of negative evidence, but in the participation literature, it is the exception. The absence of positive, or statistically significant, relationships between *relative deprivation* and support for collective action have been reported (Searles and Williams 1962; Caplan 1970; Orum 1972, chap. 4; Isaac, Mutran, and Stryker 1980, with the data for whites). In some studies, the more specific hypothesis linking status strains to right-wing politics had to be rejected (Lipset 1963, 402; Wolfringer et al. 1964; McEvoy 1971).[8] In addition, Heirich (1977) found little evidence linking stress to religious conversion, although this led him to reformulate a different stress argument. Finally, and not too surprisingly, Marx (1970) reported that strain was not a factor in *issueless* riots.

However, some of the evidence often presented as negative is far from being that clearly negative, as for instance in reports analyzed by McPhail (1971), and in Muller (1972), Grofman and Muller (1973), Crawford and Naditch (1970), and Bowen et al. (1988). Thus in a reanalysis of reports of riot participation, McPhail (1971) concluded to the absence of statistically significant relationships between relative deprivation and participation in about a third of the cases. But he reported significant, albeit allegedly "weak," relationships (with Cramer's vs of less than .30) in almost all other cases.

Similarly, Muller (1972) reported negative evidence with a measure of "long-term relative deprivation" but found a more direct, "short-term" measure of it to be significantly related.[9] Analogous remarks can be made about Grofman and Muller's (1973) reanalysis of that data set, in which four simple and direct measures of deprivation, operationalized differently than in the original study, produced substantial positive relationships (see their table 2, 523).

In the case of Crawford and Naditch (1970), their analyses bear on their own data, as well as on two other data sets. The findings with their own data reveal relatively strong positive relationships between relative deprivation and militancy (with percentage differences of about 25 percent in three of four comparisons).[10]

As for Bowan et al.'s study (1968), a reordering of their data indicates that among those expecting no "social mobility" in the future (no improvement in their position) and expressing relative satisfaction with their present position, only 25 percent manifested a high level of protest orientation. However, that proportion increased to 62 percent among the corresponding respondents expecting no mobility but expressing current relative dissatisfaction, to 48 percent among those expecting downward mobility and to 52 percent among those expecting upward mobility.[11]

On the basis of the data just presented, my own assessment is that the studies of Muller, Grofman and Muller, Crawford and Naditch, and Bowen et al. could all have been added to the confirmation list reported above. The same holds for many of the riot survey reports reviewed by McPhail. I will, however, let the reader decide on these "controversial" findings.

At any rate, the reader will have noticed that some of the negative results and all the controversial ones just reviewed involve the effects of relative deprivation. But in a review of over 350 studies, Smith and Ortiz (2002) found that many of the weak results obtained with relative deprivation variables were due to improper measures. When measures of *group* rather than *personal* relative deprivation were used, the research consistently led to very strong positive results. This led the authors to assert that group measures were the relevant ones in the explanation of collective action.

Emergence Studies

Let us turn from studies of participation to studies bearing on the emergence of collective action. The latter are typically based on the analysis, not of individual data, but of sets of events, usually representing elementary forms of collective action, such as riots, strikes, and demonstrations, although more elaborate forms of action, such as social movements and civil wars, are at times considered. The data are usually made up of either time-series for a given area, leading to *longitudinal analyses*, or of a set of events across many areas, leading to *cross-sectional ecological analyses*. Typically, the independent variables are derived from *aggregate ecological data*.

LONGITUDINAL STUDIES

With regard to longitudinal studies, the list of quantitative studies is not too long. But positive results regarding the hypothesis that deprivation was related to the occurrence of collective action have been reported in some studies, and more so in recent times (Hovland and Sears 1940; Mintz 1946; Gamson 1975; White 1989; Beck and Tolnay 1990; Jenkins, Jacobs, and Agnone 2003).[12] There were, however, studies in which the deprivation hypothesis was either not supported or only weakly supported, but mostly in earlier ones (Snyder and Tilly 1972; Tilly, Tilly, and Tilly 1975; Jenkins and Perrow 1977; Frank and Kelly 1977, 1979).[13] These results, incidentally, turned out to be influential in the negative views of American structuralists concerning the role of deprivation. But notice that often in the latter studies, many types of collective violence were lumped together, while, except for Gamson (1975), this was not the case in the set of more recent longitudinal studies reporting positive results; these concerned specific forms of conflict, that is ethnic ones. We shall also return to this issue.

It must be added that, as in the case of participation research, a large number of mainly qualitative studies bearing on the emergence of many political and social movements in the United States and Canada since at least the beginning of the twentieth century showed that they often occurred during hard economic times (for reviews of the evidence, see Lipset 1950, 1960; Pinard 1975, chap. 3) or among "lower-class" groups subjected to harsh economic conditions (Piven and Cloward 1979).

Second, there is a vast literature bearing on the occurrence of another specific type of conflict, that is, industrial strikes, particularly for the post–World War Two period. It is beyond the scope of this chapter to present a detailed review of that literature (but see Kennan 1986), since strike behaviour was increasingly approaching institutionalized forms. Let me first mention that Kennan's summary of many US studies for the long period extending from 1915 to 1980 presented "fairly convincing evidence of procyclical fluctuations in the frequency of strikes" (1125), with the number of strikes gradually increasing during the set of ascending phases of business cycles to gradually decreasing during the set of declining phases. Other studies, relying instead on regression analysis, repeatedly found that since World War Two strike frequency[14] was likely to increase in good times, when unemployment was low but when real wages were declining – that is, in line with our model, when workers faced wage deprivations but when the economic incentives were positive, as bargaining opportunities were improving in good times.[15] Such findings have been reported for long periods of the postwar period in many countries (see for instance Ashenfelter and Johnson 1969; Snyder 1975, 1977; Pencavel 1970; Shorey 1977; D.A. Smith 1972; Walsh 1975; M.R. Smith 1979, 1981; Kennan 1986). Hibbs (1976) also reported similar findings in a study aggregating data from ten advanced industrial countries. Some contrary evidence (with all or some of the regression coefficients having wrong signs and/or failing to reach statistical significance) was however reported for that period or parts of it (e.g., Cousineau and Lacroix 1976; Snyder 1975, 1977; Smith 1981; Franzosi 1995).

For the pre-war period, the evidence relying on similar regressions, with data reaching as far back as 1870 and bearing on many countries, is more limited. It is also inconsistent (Snyder 1975, 1977), owing to allegedly unfavourable institutional settings (unstable union membership, the weak political position of labour, a lack of institutionalization of collective bargaining). However, in addition to the positive evidence from business cycles for the U.S., bearing in part on the pre-war period and summarized by Kennan, Shorey (1977) presented positive evidence for Great Britain. Moreover Snyder's (1975) negative evidence for France for the period 1876 to 1937 runs contrary (despite his claim) to the positive findings of Shorter and Tilly (1974, 96ff.) for about the same period (1890–1938).[16]

This is not to overlook the fact that major strike waves did occur in some countries during depression periods, as in France and the United States during the 1930s, when, despite high levels of unemployment, workers mobilized, presumably because of favourable political opportunities (Tarrow 1998, 72–3). In response to wage cuts and longer hours, unionization drives were increasingly taking place, and more and more strikes involved union recognition, reaching about 50 percent in 1934 and after (Piven and Cloward 1979, chap. 3; see also Snyder 1977). But notice that the peak of strikes between 1933 and 1938 occurred in 1937, at the peak of that business cycle (Jurkat and Jurkat 1949, reported by Kennan 1986, table 19.1).

CROSS-SECTIONAL ECOLOGICAL STUDIES

Turning to ecological *cross-sectional* (usually cross-national) studies of collective action, there are, first, studies *aggregating many types of collective violence*, which have often been carried out by authors linked to the relative deprivation perspective. Their results have been very supportive of the deprivation hypothesis, despite serious methodological problems to be discussed later (Gurr 1968; Feierabend and Feierabend 1972; Gurr and Duvall 1973). The most sophisticated ecological work of that type, bearing on more than one hundred nations, is that of Hibbs (1973). Although his conclusions failed to support a relative deprivation hypothesis, which was more strictly cast than Gurr's or the Feierabends' hypotheses, his results were nevertheless positive when the analysis included as direct or indirect factors of mass political violence many measures of absolute deprivation or satisfaction, such as the level of economic development, changes in affluence, and group discrimination on ethnic, religious, or other communal lines. Support for the deprivation hypothesis in other collective violence studies was also found by Markoff (1985) and Muller and Seligson (1987).[17]

In studies of *specific forms of collective action or social movements*, positive results concerning deprivation were reported by Jenkins (1982) in an ecological analysis of peasant rebellions in Russia.[18] Positive results were also reported in ecological research on various types of US movements: the Townsend movement (Amenta and Zyler 1991), the North Carolina Farmers' Alliance and People's Party (Redding 1992), the patriot/militia movement of the 1990s (Van Dyke and Soule 2002), and homeless protest of the 1980s (Snow, Soule, and Cress 2005). McCarthy and his collaborators (1988) did, however, find that grievances were not a factor in the formation of American groups opposing drunk driving. But notice that in that study, grievances – having been a victim of drunk driving – were a very important factor of participation among members and even more so among leaders of the groups.

Turning to *ethnic collective action* specifically, Gurr (1993b) found that, in a world-wide study of more than two hundred groups, grievances and mobilization together were factors of communal (mostly ethnic) protest and rebellion. But Koopmans' (1996) data on racist and extreme right violence in Western Europe did not support the notion that deprivations were sufficient to explain that violence, although the author appears to accept that it could be necessary, in conjunction with opportunities; but no multivariate analyses were carried out.

Finally, a large number of cross-sectional ecological studies have been carried out regarding American Black urban riots during the 1960s, in order to assess whether these riots were more likely to occur, or were more likely to be severe, in communities characterized by high levels of deprivation than in others. Recall that many studies of individual participation in riots, as seen above, supported the deprivation hypothesis (e.g., Sears and McConahay 1970; Paige 1971; also the studies reviewed by McPhail (1971), discussed above). One of the best studies in this regard (Paige 1971) showed that political grievances (distrust of the local government to do what is right) exerted very strong effects on riot participation, but only in interaction with high political efficacy (a disposition close to expectancy of success in our model). Conversely those high on grievances but low on efficacy were the least likely participants.[19]

However, in some ecological riot studies, the evidence is negative, even though for earlier periods some positive, but limited, evidence had been presented (Lieberson and Silverman 1965; Bloombaum 1968). While at the zero-order level, many indicators of deprivations appeared to be related to riot frequency and severity for the 1960s (e.g., Downes 1968), most studies relying on multivariate analysis reported that these relationships tended to vanish when controls were introduced for region (the South vs. the rest) and for community size or size of the Black population (Spilerman 1970, 1971, 1976; Downes 1970; Ford and Moore 1970; Jiobu 1971; Lieske 1978). In this series of studies, there is only limited evidence linking riot severity to deprivation (Wanderer 1969; Morgan and Clark 1973) or linking riot frequency to deprivation (Jiobu 1974). Notice, incidentally, that in at least the last two studies cited, as well as in Lieske (1978), the results indicated that communities with a larger number of poor Blacks were less likely to experience riots or severe riots than those above the poverty level, a finding analogous to the negative poverty-participation relationship discussed earlier. It is worth mentioning that in general the authors of this set of studies were not led by their negative findings to reject altogether deprivation as a motivating factor. Spilerman (1970), for instance, suggested instead that there was geographic uniformity in the impact of the grievances entertained by Black Americans (see also Orum's argument 1972, 76, and Ladner et al.'s 1981). Finally community differences in riot frequency or severity may be more related to variations in structural conduciveness than variations in deprivation (see the interesting work of Snyder 1979 in this regard).

In more recent studies of these urban riots, Olzak and Shanahan (1996) and Myers (1997) rejected deprivation hypotheses with most indicators, in favour of competition arguments. But notice first that, as in some studies just cited, many of their negative results about deprivation involved measures of poverty, again something discussed earlier. Both studies, however, reported an important exception. In the first study, the authors reported that the percentage of nonwhite males unemployed yielded very positive effects. Myers reported similar results with the number of nonwhite unemployed. Both studies, however, used these unemployment measures as part of their competition, rather than deprivation, indicators. As with Useem (1998), it can be asserted that these results could be just as well, if not more so, interpreted as supporting deprivation arguments.

In recent years, many quantitative cross-national ecological studies of civil wars during the second half of the last century

raised the question of whether ethnic diversity or ethnic grievances were important factors for civil wars in general and for
ethnic civil wars in particular, both claims having often been
made by students of nationalism. So far, these investigations
have yielded contradictory results. For instance, Fearon and
Laitin (2003), Collier and Hoeffler (2004), and Fearon, Kasara,
and Laitin (2007) reached the conclusions that ethnic diversity,
discrimination, minority group dominance, or other grievances
were very poor predictors of civil wars in general or even of ethnic civil wars, stressing instead the role of "greed" among rebels
as internal motives and of potential economic gains as external
incentives. Conversely, studies by Sambanis (2001), Cederman
and Girardin (2007), Buhaug, Cederman, and Rod (2008), and
Wimmer, Cederman, and Min (2009) reached partly opposite
conclusions, showing in particular that if ethnic diversity was
again of minor significance, ethnic political exclusion was a very
powerful determinant of civil wars. The evidence of this second
group of authors is definitely more convincing. Their conclusions were reached at times by disaggregating ethnic from other
civil wars and, above all, in the case of the last three studies, by
relying on much better measures of political exclusion.[20] In particular, Buhaud and his co-authors disaggregated national-level
data into multiple center-periphery dyads, considering the power
balance between each dyad of politically excluded ethnic groups
and the dominant one(s). And Wimmer and his colleagues
insisted that one ought to consider the modern state as an essential actor in such conflicts and that it was necessary to disaggregate various ethnopolitical configurations of state power and the
types of conflict they generated.[21] Notice that in these studies,
both political grievances (exclusion) and human resources (the
relative or absolute size of the excluded group) increased the
probability of at least some types of violent conflict.

THE EVIDENCE REGARDING THE IMPACT OF EMOTIONS

There is much less evidence concerning the role of emotions in
action participation. Originally that evidence was largely drawn

from qualitative studies (e.g., Taylor 1995; Gould 2004), but now evidence is also starting to emerge from quantitative studies (Van Zomeren et al. 2004; Klandermans, Van der Toorn, and Van Stekelenburg 2008). Contrary to the evidence on grievances, the evidence regarding emotions is, however, neither inconsistent nor controversial; it is, as expected, always positive.

SUMMARY

The hypothesis regarding the role of grievances was largely supported by a detailed examination of the available evidence. It was shown first that in the research bearing on individual participation in and support of protest, usually bearing on a single movement or episode of collective action, the supporting evidence is very substantial indeed, even if in some instances the relationships did not appear overly strong, for reasons to be examined in the next chapter. The presumed negative evidence was, however, often casual and selective. Second, with regard to quantitative, longitudinal ecological studies, we observed that those inspired by the resource mobilization perspective produced evidence unsupportive of the deprivation hypothesis, although this was in studies aggregating many different types of "collective violence," a problem also to be considered. But some positive evidence from time-series analyses of ethnic protest, a specific type of contention, has been reported. The same holds generally regarding time-series analyses of industrial conflict, particularly for the post-World War Two period. Finally cross-sectional ecological studies of the emergence of protest, particularly those bearing on specific types of collective action, generally yielded positive evidence, except for the conflicting results regarding American race riots and civil wars.

What can be made of the conflicting evidence often reported? It will be argued that these contradictions are related to methodological problems, some bearing on data and measurement issues, others on the types of analytical design adopted. The most serious problems involve basic principles of the logic of inquiry. These are the issues to be examined in the next chapter.

3

Methodological Problems Invalidating Some Research on Grievances

While engaged in a review of the evidence, I was struck by recurring methodological problems affecting parts of the research. These at times concerned typical data and measurement problems, something recurrently found in empirical work of any kind. But more serious problems of faulty analytical designs could be observed in a particular type of research, which is increasingly common in the field. Let us start with the first type of problems.

DATA AND MEASUREMENT PROBLEMS

Among the data and measurement problems, there were first those pertaining to the dependent variables, that is, various forms of contentious collective action. It is evident that with regard to the emergence of such action, it is preferable to work from many collective action episodes across a set of places and/or, even preferably, across long time periods instead of from single episodes.

However, as has too often been done, the aggregation of many different types of protest, under general categories such as "civil strife" or "collective violence" tends to generate serious problems, unless one has solid grounds to assume that they are produced by the very same determinants. But precisely such an assumption is generally untenable. There are good a priori reasons to believe that food riots, tax rebellions, land seizures, violent strikes, political demonstrations, insurrections, coups, and revolutions do not all respond to the same grievances but mainly to *relevant* deprivations, that is, to those that the action aims at eliminating. If this is so, these different types of contention should not all be lumped together and related to, say, food prices or real wages, in order to test deprivation hypotheses, as, for instance, the Tillys and Gurr, among others, have too easily done (e.g., Tilly, Tilly, and Tilly 1975, 81; Gurr 1970).[1] What if, for instance, tax rebellions were first a "reactive" response to tax exactions rather than to rising food prices, to belabour the obvious? Again if many types of political unrest increase with unemployment, but industrial conflict decreases with it, the aggregation of these forms of collective action, as done by Snyder and Tilly (1972), is bound to work against a deprivation hypothesis measured by levels of unemployment. Conversely, if the factors favoured by some of these authors (e.g., organization or opportunities) bear similar relationships to all the aggregated forms of collective action, the hypotheses regarding these factors are bound to fare well.

Even when one considers only one type of collective action, the analysis may soon reveal the necessity to distinguish sub-types. Shorter and Tilly (1974, chap. 4), for instance, distinguished offensive strikes, aiming at gaining new grounds for workers, from defensive ones carried out to resist speedups, wage cuts, or impositions of new work rules. Thus the two types appear to be responding to different kinds of motives, and indeed the authors present findings showing that for a period for which such data were available, the two types of strikes did bear strong opposite correlations to their independent variables (see table 4.6), and in particular, that only the offensive strikes bear the expected relationships to real wages (negative) and to economic prosperity (positive). But rather than carrying out different regression analyses for these two types of strikes, whenever the data were available, we find the distinction altogether dropped from their analyses, and then completely absent from Snyder's (1975) analysis of the same data.[2]

Let us now turn to the independent variables. First, surveys of individuals are obviously better than ecological studies for measuring internal motives such as deprivations and, in particular, felt grievances; conversely socio-economic characteristics relied upon in ecological studies are poor predictors of feelings of discontent (Muller and Jukam 1983). This again should work to the detriment of grievances hypotheses in this last type of studies. But even in survey research, researchers often fail to measure the relevant deprivations or to assess if given conditions are actually the sources of felt grievances. Concerning the first point, Cantril's self-anchoring scale has, for instance, been widely used to measure relative deprivation in studies of racial protest by American Blacks. But while Matthews and Prothro (1966) used it to appropriately measure racial deprivation, Bowen et al. (1968) and Crawford and Naditch (1970) used it to simply measure their general personal life conditions. This is not too serious if one follows traditional relative deprivation theory, which states that any type of frustration (relevant or displaced) can equally lead to any form of aggression. My own hypothesis, however, states that while all forms of deprivations can occasionally trigger participation, the relevant ones will by far be the most important for practically all participants, and the essential ones for the emergence of protest. In addition, as was mentioned, group relative deprivations, not personal ones, clearly turned out to be the relevant ones in the large-scale analysis of Smith and Ortiz (2002).

The problem is even more serious in ecological studies. First, you often wonder to what extent the available ecological measures retained really tap deprivation as such, let alone relative deprivation, as for instance in Snyder and Tilly's (1972) index of prices of manufactured goods (without wage data), in Gurr's (1968) measure of religious cleavages, or in Fearon and Laitin's (2003) and in Collier and Hoeffler's (2004) measures of ethnic/linguistic diversity. Religious and ethnic diversity, for instance, do not necessarily imply deprivations. Second, for many types of grievances, there are unfortunately no obvious ecological measures, and therefore researchers have tended to rely all too often on economic or class measures as if they were the most relevant ones (e.g., in Tilly's and in the Feierabends' data sets, in Olzak and Shanahan's and in Myers' analyses of Black riots). By contrast, in most studies of participation in ethnic movements, cited earlier, the measures of ethnic deprivations were much more likely to tap felt grievances. In the absence of such good measures in ecological studies, one should not assume that any other type of presumed deprivation could do as a substitute.[3] In particular, in many instances the most relevant deprivations regarding political violence could very well be political rather than economic, and indeed political grievances, when used, were shown to be powerful predictors of protest. Among the cases cited, see for instance Paige's (1971) study of riots, the many studies of collective violence carried out by Muller and his colleagues after 1980, and the recent studies of civil wars in which positive deprivation effects were obtained.

Third, the collectivities for which the data are aggregated are generally too large. Disturbances in one locality or region in reaction to, say, local or regional political grievances are not necessarily going to be related to measures of national political conditions, let alone to national measures of altogether different kinds of deprivations.[4] It is revealing that in his study of riot participation in Newark, New Jersey, Paige (1971) relied on really relevant grievances, that is, absolute political deprivation against the local government. I am of course aware that often no better data are available, but an essential point remains: if one cannot be sure of the validity of the measures, one cannot be sure of the validity of the conclusions either. Much greater sensitivity to which groups are affected by which problems in which places at what time is certainly warranted. Finally, the research is at times based on indicators that comprise so many diverse elements and become so complex that one wonders what they are measuring, as for instance in Gurr and Duvall's (1973) strain index. It contains so many indicators that one remains uncertain about the specific factors producing the effects, if any.

All in all, it can be suggested that many of the data and measurement problems raised are at least partially responsible for the negative or weak results regarding the role of deprivation reported in the studies reviewed, as well as in others. More refined approaches are needed to validly ascertain whether the deprivation hypothesis is supported or not.

PROBLEMS OF ANALYTICAL DESIGNS

A more serious source of inconsistency in the findings concerning the impact of deprivation may lie in an altogether different direction, that is, in the ways in which the data analyses have been carried out. Usually, as recognized by Snyder (1978), the theories in this field present sophisticated frameworks in which deprivation, if at all considered, is but one factor among others. Whether one considers the theories of Blumer, Turner and Killian, Smelser, Gurr, or Tilly, and their associates, one finds *multidimensional* models. Those who have not developed such models are really the exceptions (e.g., Davies, the Feierabends). In particular, both Smelser's and Tilly's theories consider that deprivations or interests, respectively, are but one in a larger set of determinants. Both of them see mobilization as an important factor. Moreover, in the case of Smelser, the model, and rightly so, is explicitly *multiplicative,* involving *interactions*: all determinants are necessary for collective behaviour to occur. Indeed the same is implicit in Tilly's mobilization model (Snyder 1978, 520) and, in addition, that model considers the possibility of interdependence between the components of the model. Even Gurr and Duvall (1973) have modified an earlier model to introduce interdependence and some degree of interaction in their new formulation.

Unfortunately, a large part of this sophistication tends to be absent from the empirical work inspired by those theories.[5] Research carried out along the lines of the early approaches rarely fails to investigate the role of deprivation but often fails to investigate the other factors, thus making it easier for critics to picture these theories as deprivation-only models. In participation studies, when factors other than deprivation are considered, researchers have tended to limit themselves to measures of organization (e.g., union membership) or of social integration. Mobilization exposure in particular is practically never measured.

But even when other factors are considered, the tendency has been to work with additive models only. Indeed, empirical investigations involving also the examination of interaction effects between motivation and structural factors are extremely rare in both surveys and ecological studies. There are but very few exceptions (Gurr and Duvall 1973; Hibbs 1973; Jiobu 1974; Pinard 1975; LeCavalier 1983; Muller and Seligson 1987). Some participation studies did consider interactions, not between motivation and some structural components, but only between some of the components of motivation, such as deprivation and incentives (Paige 1971; Klandermans 1984; Pinard and Hamilton 1986; Opp 1988; Muller, Dietz, and Finkel 1991; Roefs, Klandermans, and Olivier 1998; and Finkel and Muller 1998).

But if research following the early approaches also frequently manifested the shortcomings just mentioned, how can we explain that it nevertheless usually uncovered positive relationships, and often strong ones, between deprivation and participation in collective action? The answer, it is claimed, is relatively simple: although researchers in those traditions generally failed to measure separately and control for mobilization, their analyses were nevertheless on the whole valid if it can be assumed that, first, mobilization efforts had been exerted, at least to some extent, and second, that these efforts had been constant over time or uniform over the entire population investigated. Under such conditions, the control of mobilization was not required. The first assumption – the presence of mobilizing efforts – was usually valid in those studies, since researchers were generally analyzing social movements that for some time had exerted mobilization efforts towards the entire population sampled. Hence the frequent finding of positive deprivation/participation relationships. Moreover, if the situation is one of substantial mobilization efforts, then the relationships observed should be strong; if not, they should be much weaker.[6]

The second assumption – that these efforts had been constant or ubiquitous – may have been valid in most participation studies, as well as in some cross-sectional ecological studies of specific forms of collective action or social movements reviewed earlier. Hence their positive findings regarding deprivation. But that second assumption may have been invalid in other cross-sectional studies. This would constitute another reason for the not infrequent discovery of relatively weak and/or non-significant relationships.[7] An analogous set of arguments holds for Jenkins (1982) and for Lieberson and Silverman's (1965) cross-sectional ecological studies.[8]

Positive results of cross-sectional ecological studies by Gurr, the Feierabends, and Hibbs do, however, appear surprising. Clearly one cannot assume mobilization, not measured here either, to have been present and constant across the hundred or so countries of their "samples." Therefore, how could they obtain positive deprivation/incidence relationships, even if not always large? There are a great many characteristics that distinguish the more and less deprived (developed) countries of the world and that could be found to be related to political instability. This renders the identification of any real determinant difficult. But one possibility is that mobilization would be more likely to be present in the less developed countries, owing to larger permanent pools of alienated organizations and of ideological dissidents. Hence, given that you have here very large differences in levels of deprivation and that it can be postulated that these positively co-vary, at least to a moderate degree, with levels of mobilization, one is bound to observe the deprivation/incidence relationships hypothesized.

Turning to the longitudinal studies of researchers from the political process perspective, some of their results concerning deprivation were either negative or very weak, as seen above, particularly when many types of collective action were aggregated into single measures of collective violence. To the extent that the theories to which these analyses were addressed were multidimensional, interactive ones, these analyses manifested, however, two major flaws. First, while their analyses had at times the merit of being multivariate, they, however, also usually failed to control for mobilization, which could not be assumed to have been present and constant over long periods. This failure to control for mobilization is surprising given the central role attributed to this factor in their theories and the fact that the appearance of mobilization is seen as problematic under conditions of deprivation or interest, as was rightly assumed in those theories (e.g., Snyder and Tilly 1972, 526; Snyder 1978, 504–5).

Table 3.1
Collective Protest over Two Hundred Years, by Mobilization and Deprivation
(percentages)

Mobilization:	Present		Absent	
Relevant Deprivation:	Present	Absent	Present	Absent
Incidence of a type of protest:				
Yes	50	0	0	0
No	50	100	100	100
Number of Years	(20)	(5)	(80)	(95)

Indeed the best of the ecological studies usually end up with the measurement of about the same limited set of factors, that is, deprivation, coercion-repression, and organization.[9]

That mobilization could not have been assumed to be present and constant is manifestly the case in the longitudinal studies of collective violence: mobilization, for instance, could obviously not be so assumed in France from 1830 to 1960. In studies of those phenomena (Snyder and Tilly 1972; Tilly, Tilly, and Tilly 1975), the only variables measured – and very remotely at that – were again the three variables just mentioned, and in the multivariate analysis involving them, the models used were only additive ones.[10]

The problem caused by such a failure is best illustrated with the following tabulations based on an hypothetical longitudinal study. In table 3.1, the incidence of collective protest over two hundred years is assumed to be related to both deprivation and mobilization. In this hypothetical but realistic example, all variables, for the sake of simplicity, are assumed to be either present or absent. Half the years are assumed to be years of deprivation, but mobilization, a problematic and rare occurrence, is assumed to occur in only a fifth of those years. Moreover, the model involves interaction, both factors being necessary (though not sufficient). Finally the model assumes that mobilization is more likely to develop during years of deprivation. Under such conditions, one should observe in table 3.1 that both factors are necessary for collective protest to occur. It is important to notice that, by analogy, participation studies and some cross-sectional

Table 3.2
Collective Protest over Two Hundred Years, by Deprivation (percentages)

Relevant Deprivation:	Present	Absent
Incidence of a type of protest:		
Yes	10	0
No	90	100
Number of Years	(100)	(100)

ecological studies tend to consider only the left-hand quadrant of that table, in which mobilization is assumed to be present. In that quadrant one can easily observe a strong deprivation effect.

But longitudinal studies are not so limited, since all time periods are considered, whether mobilization was present or not. The failure to control for mobilization, however, results in a collapse of the two quadrants into a single one, yielding the weak deprivation effect shown in table 3.2.[11]

In short, since in "good" longitudinal studies, many years of deprivation without mobilization are lumped together with fewer years of deprivation with mobilization, the deprivation effect, hypothesized to be taking place only under mobilization, becomes very weak; but that result is now spurious. The sole theories that their tests allow them to reject are the simplistic deprivation-only theories. As already mentioned, I concur with them in this rejection.

The tests of the longitudinal studies, unfortunately, also manifest at times a second flaw. They are designed to measure the effect of fluctuations in the independent variables, not the impact of the stable states of these variables. But given an interaction model, it is possible for the yearly fluctuations in a dependent variable to be triggered by fluctuations in only one independent variable, with the others being simply present and constant; for instance, you could have a period during which deprivation and organization would both be present and constant but during which increases in mobilization efforts would trigger collective violence. With the statistical models employed and given the period studied, the only effect that could be detected in this instance would be the triggering effect of mobilization; but this would obviously not mean that the other factors did not also need to be present. To test for that, one would ideally need a longer period during which all factors would manifest fluctuations and certainly an analysis of interaction effects.

Consider, for instance, conflicts between ethnic groups, with each group being highly organized and in a long-lasting relationship of super-ordination and subordination. Such conflicts, for instance, could at times be triggered by new external incentives increasing mobilization levels among the subordinates. Conversely, they could at times be triggered by increasing deprivations under conditions of high organization on the part of the subordinate people.[12] In the first example, only incentives and mobilization would appear as determinants if one carried out the type of analysis just reviewed. In the second example, only deprivation would appear as an important factor. Both conclusions would obviously be wrong.[13]

SUMMARY AND CONCLUSION

The arguments of this chapter can be briefly summarized. A critical examination of the contradictory evidence led me to raise many issues regarding both measurement and analytical design problems and to suggest that these problems were responsible for much of the negative evidence. The problems identified included the frequent undue aggregation of different types of collective action, in particular in longitudinal studies, the questionable measurement of deprivations, particularly in those studies and in cross-sectional studies of civil wars, the absence of measurement of the essential mobilization factor, with the serious consequences this entailed for studies of emergence, and finally, the quasi-exclusive use of additive, rather than multiplicative, models. Deprivation, it was asserted, is but one of the factors of an appropriate multidimensional, interactive model, and fluctuations in any one of them, or in only some of them, could be the triggering factor or factors of new outbreaks, as long as the other factors were also present. Contrary to a central claim of the political process approach, there is ample evidence that grievances, in particular, can at times be one of the triggering factors. In short all this leads to the conclusion that the deprivation hypothesis must remain a central concern on the research agenda.

In the next chapter, a detailed examination of other motivating components, in particular aspirations and moral obligations, collective and selective incentives, and expectancy of success will be carried out. This will then lead in chapter 5 to the elaboration of a general motivation model, as a synthesis of the disparate models found in the literature and integrating all internal motives (grievances, aspirations, and moral obligations), as well as external incentives (collective as well as selective) and expectancy of success.

4

Other Motivational Components

In previous chapters, the deprivations versus interests controversy was shown to rest on theoretical confusions and ambiguities, on a selective reading of the evidence regarding deprivations, and on severe methodological flaws observed in that evidence. So far the important conclusion reached was that there were many reasons to support a strong, although not exclusive, deprivation or grievance hypothesis.

In this chapter, we turn to an examination of other relevant motivational components. First, the role of aspirations, another internal motive, one that is also controversial albeit much neglected, will be examined. After that the motivational components underlying the dominant structural approaches, that is, external incentives, both collective and selective, will be considered. A subsequent discussion of the notions of ideologies and solidarities will lead us to introduce moral obligations as a third internal motive. Finally, the third major motivational component, expectancy of success, which has too often been neglected, will be introduced.

For this discussion, additional key definitions will be needed. While deprivations, as seen previously, refer to an individual's disadvantages or other conditions that may possibly result in suffering and lead to feelings of grievances, simple *aspirations*, on the other hand, refer to an individual's desires for some potential goods, collective or selective, not considered as having been unjustly denied to him or her. Such desires are, therefore, by definition, not the result of deprivations.

On the other hand, *external collective incentives* are defined as the collective goods or bads (or public goods or bads) the benefits or costs of which cannot be withheld from, or avoided by, members of a collectivity who did not contribute to obtaining or avoiding them.[1] Thus, one should consider the net positive or negative returns of these incentives. Conversely *selective incentives or private rewards* can be defined as benefits that accrue only to a group's members who are making contributions to the provision of a collective good, while *selective disincentives* are personal costs incurred by members making contributions. Thus, one can think of *net* selective incentives or *net* personal costs, notions at times left implicit. These rewards and costs could be material, such as financial support, career benefits, leadership positions, financial costs, physical pains or threats, imprisonment, and so on, or often social, such as status rewards or costs, praise, love or friendship ties or social rejection, new experiences, and so on, not to mention the emotional pleasures and excitement accompanying demonstrations or ritual activities.

Third, *moral obligations* are another type of internal forces pushing one to action out of altruism, of a sense of duty dictating selfless contributions to some collective action. Finally, *expectancies of success* bear on the felt probabilities that intermediate or ultimate goals will be reached.

ASPIRATIONS AS INTERNAL MOTIVES

Aspirations are rarely considered explicitly as a motive in the general theories of contentious collective action. It can be claimed that they remain an important element of motivation, that specifically, with grievances, they constitute a second internal motive pushing one to contentious collective action.[2] Let us examine this claim.[3]

Perspectives on the Role of Aspirations

What perspectives on aspirations does one find in the literature? Basically, aspiration is the internal motive, the presence of which is often implicitly assumed among authors whose motivation model rests simply on "interests," these referring to the collective goods pursued. In some fields, aspirations are even considered as the sole or at least the dominant internal motive. This is particularly frequent in the work of economists, but this is not surprising, given that their concerns bear mainly on routine collective action and that such action is more likely to exhibit such a motivational pattern (e.g., Olson 1965). Some of Raymond Breton's studies also implicitly rest mainly on group aspirations. This is particularly the case with his analysis of the so-called Quiet Revolution, which took place in Quebec during the 1960s and 1970s, a period of very rapid modernization after a long period of stagnating institutional arrangements. This new period created opportunities for widespread and intensive confrontations over the redistribution of power and influence in a large number of institutions. The contention remained, however, largely elite-based and mostly carried out through routine institutions, although it also contributed to the emergence of intense conflict between the independentist and federalist camps and, for a time, of violent confrontations with the marginal Front de libération du Québec (Breton 1972).

In labour relations, which have become increasingly institutionalized, simple aspirations, again for collective goods, could at times be a dominant motive leading workers, otherwise relatively satisfied, to nevertheless launch strikes to improve their conditions during favourable economic conditions (for instances of this, see Smith 1981, 381; Franzosi 1995, chap. 2). However, subsequent uncompromising responses by employers could greatly increase motivation by adding grievances to such aspirations.

But for some authors, aspirations are even seen as the sole motive in non-institutionalized confrontations. For instance, in their empirical study of civil wars, reviewed in chapter 2, Collier and Hoeffler's (2004) made an explicit recourse to strong aspirations – "greed" was the term they used – among rebels and rejected the role of grievances altogether. Similar views on aspiration, although implicit, can be observed among some proponents of the competition model of ethnic conflict, for whom the motivation factor rests only on interests and who reject any grievance argument (Nielsen 1985; also Nagel and Olzak 1982). The perspectives of all these authors have however been empirically challenged.[4] Notice that while challenging the greed perspective in the analysis of all civil wars, Wimmer, Cederman, and Min (2009) maintained, as mentioned before, that competition, and implicitly aspirations, were the underlying motives in one type of such wars, that is, wars involving infighting within ethnically divided ruling elites; but this was a rare type in their data.[5]

Other authors do tend to consider both aspirations and grievances as internal motives in the initiation of any contentious action, placing the insistence on one or the other, although their relative weight usually remains vague. This can be observed among social scientists working within the political process/contentious politics approach. Thus, while in his definition of interest Tilly (1978) explicitly restricts it to external collective incentives, he at times, as was seen, slips into triple notions of "interests, grievances, and aspirations" or the like. But this always remains unelaborated and in practice interests as external incentives conflate any internal motive, with aspirations for collective goods often implied. One can also find a model of communal conflict based on both aspirations and grievances in Melson and Wolpe (1970). They argue that modernization and communal social mobilization generate communal economic, status, and power aspirations among large numbers of citizens, which in turn lead to communal competition with unequal outcomes, in particular the blocking of these aspirations among some of the groups, all of this resulting in grievances and conflict.

A frequent pattern, according to some authors, is that grievance motives are important for most participants, but that they come in combination with aspirations for some special collective and/or selective goods among some segments of the elites. Thus, in his theory of ethnic conflict in the Third World, Horowitz (1971, 1985) stresses status (group worth) and territorial grievances shared by both masses and elites, but also, secondarily, specific aspirations for civil service and university positions within the young educated elites, which turn out to symbolize the above grievances and can themselves be transformed into

grievances if they are blocked. The same type of argument under-
lies Breton and Stasiulis's (1980) analysis of the francophone-
anglophone conflict in Canada, in which the economic, status,
and power inequalities for the general Francophone population
are juxtaposed to the (implicit) aspirations of politicians and
bureaucrats over the distribution of governmental power (compare their chapters 3.2, 3.3, and 3.8 with chapter 3.5; see also
Breton 1998). In a study of a right-wing political protest movement, in which supporters were primarily motivated by economic grievances, the analysis further revealed that the easier
recruitment of "notables" as party candidates under improved
electoral opportunities could be mainly interpreted not by shared
grievances with other supporters but by their aspirations for the
selective political and status incentives involved in the position
of elected MPs (Pinard 1975, 124ff.).

Similarly, in his historical analyses of state breakdowns, Goldstone (1991) observed both high levels of distress in the general
population and of threats among established elites, but also high
aspirations for power among new rising elites, to be followed by
grievances if they faced exclusion. In an analysis of the Quebec
independence movement, it was found that francophone provincial government employees were much more likely supporters
of sovereignty than other francophone government employees,
especially federal ones, the latter being the least likely supporters
(Kowalchuk and Pinard 1993). Presumably the first had, in addition to grievances similar to those of other francophones, special
aspirations for the larger employment pool that independence
would necessarily create at what is now the provincial government level. In the same vein, Oberschall (1973) developed an
interesting analysis of the specific risk/reward ratios faced by
leaders from various occupational groups, in this case to account
for both the negative and the positive inducements to activism in
opposition movements. It is important to realize that in all these
analyses of elites or leaders, the prevailing aspirations are not
only for selective goods, as is often implied, but also for special
collective ones. These participants aspire to better collective conditions for their own subgroup, as well as to selective rewards
for themselves.

In their economic theory of social movements, which relies on the demand and supply analogy, Breton and Breton (1969) argue that the people's demand for movements is entirely motivated by relative deprivations, but that their supply comes from social entrepreneurs who, spurred by the opportunities the demand generates, simply aspire to reap selective incentives of monetary, prestige, or power dimensions. In that model, ordinary constituency members making demands and the entrepreneurs trying to meet them have completely different motives, somewhat like in McCarthy and Zald's (1973) professional social movements. In Breton and Breton's subsequent study of Canadian disunity (1980), the perspective is altered. The contention is now viewed as involving exclusively organizational elites struggling over the distribution of organizational power, with the masses remaining uninvolved. These elites' motivation rests on both strong aspirations for positions within the organizational elites and for accession to organizational power, and on grievances generated by the presence of linguistic and regional barriers to the accession to these positions and power. The hypothesis proposed is that in that case these grievances rather than aspirations are likely to be the main motives driving challengers towards contentious forms of action; otherwise why would they not pursue their aspirations through institutionalized means?

The Role of Aspirations Assessed

The review of this literature, as well as previous discussions, lead us to the following propositions. First, it is important to distinguish aspirations for collective goods from aspirations for selective rewards. Aspirations are likely to be the almost exclusive internal motive for obtaining *selective* incentives, in routine as well as in contentious collective action. These aspirations might involve desires for personal rewards during one's contributions to the action (e.g., peer approval, social prestige, economic retributions), as well as after the pursued goals have been reached (e.g., permanent employment, patronage).

Conversely, simple aspirations for collective goods are likely to be predominant only in the more routine forms of collective action, as argued in the work of Olson, R. Breton, Smith, and Franzosi, some of which was just briefly reviewed. But contrary to the claims of Collier and Hoeffler, as well as of Nielsen, an alternative hypothesis is that, as one moves to increasingly contentious collective action,[6] rank and file participants will be most likely to act on the basis of their grievances, with simple aspirations playing a very secondary role, if at all.[7] For such participants, the drives flowing from feelings of unjust treatments are likely to be much stronger pushes to action than simple desires for better conditions.

Among some organizers and leaders, however, simple aspirations for the collective good could be more prevalent, but coming in combination with grievances, the latter generally remaining more important. This could be observed, for instance, among movement leaders engaging in electoral politics on the basis of both their group's political grievances and strong aspirations for increased collective power; while benefiting the entire constituency, such power could be much more important for them. In addition, aspirations alone could play the determining role among leaders who, in addition to striving for the overall goals of a movement, are also pursuing particular collective goods that are not part of the expressed goals of a movement and benefiting only their group. An example would be an activist group's aspirations for the collective pool of civil service jobs becoming available after the overthrow of governing authorities. This is indeed the reason for frequent assertions in the literature – or by opponents in contentious actions – that movement leaders are moved by their sole aspirations for collective as well as private goods, assertions most often grossly exaggerated. Here it is hypothesized that without group grievances, elite or popular aspirations would not easily move a collectivity much beyond collective action of a more routine kind.

One research problem is that aspirations are rarely if ever explicitly measured, so that their impact, contrary to that of deprivations, has rarely been empirically ascertained, except by inferences from indirect evidence. Yet aspirations should not be more difficult to measure than grievances, threats, or other attitudes once their potential role is considered. Some argue that it

would be difficult to disentangle the respective impact of grievances and aspirations when acting in combination. But measuring the presence and strength of each would go a long way in
resolving that problem.

In short, even if the impact of aspirations is not as dominant
in contentious collective action as is sometimes assumed, aspirations could be important enough, in some groups some of the
time to be taken into account in a general motivation model.

DEPRIVATIONS, INCENTIVES, PRINCIPLES, AND SOLIDARITY

The structural approaches generated debates concerning the role
of selective and collective incentives and of values, ideologies,
principles, and solidarity. These debates are not without ambiguities, not to speak of the confusions concerning the role of these
components relative to that of the internal motives previously
discussed. Let us consider these issues.

Grievances versus Collective Incentives

The first argument is that it is unsound to oppose grievances and
incentives as relevant motivating factors in contentious collective action. The proponents of structural approaches placed an
almost exclusive emphasis on incentives for such factors, given
that their attention was concentrated on mobilization problems
and on the "supply" side of social movements. Indeed to the
extent that the new focus was no longer on the recruitment of
masses but on political processes and the power struggles opposing contending groups, especially their leaders (Marx and Wood
1975, 386), the emphasis could easily shift from the masses' pre-
dicaments to the goals or objectives of these struggles, that is, to
external collective incentives. Hence grievances as forces pushing
one to pursue these goods were largely disregarded, neglecting
Tarrow's (1989a, 138) earlier assertion that people's demands, at
least in part, emerged from their grievances.

By contrast, it is argued that both felt grievances/emotions
and/or aspirations and/or moral obligations (the latter to be

examined shortly) and some forms of net external incentives are necessary motivating factors.[8] Put differently, in the same way that both the supply and demand side of social movements must be considered, both former theories stressing deprivations and structural theories stressing interests must be given due consideration. Some might argue that the internal motives (e.g., deprivations) are so closely interrelated with the collective incentives that one might dispense with considering the first.[9] But the kind of internal motives involved and their strength will greatly affect the attraction of the collective incentives, so that neglecting the first will obscure much of the motivation processes. In particular, both are separately and interactively involved in determining the utility of the action.

There is no disagreement concerning the importance of collective incentives. There should not be either concerning the emotions accompanying them, although this is only a recent concern. Moreover, no one would want to disregard both of them in accounting for contentious action. But apart from the evidence concerning strike activity, in which it was frequently found that the salience of the workers' claims increased during good economic times, there are unfortunately few studies testing the motivating role of collective incentives, since researchers in the political process approach tend to assume the presence of "interests" and their relatively constant nature in the course of the action. This generally led them not to measure interests. Regarding emotions amplifying anticipated collective gains, joy and enthusiasm are likely to develop, as well as fear regarding anticipated losses (Aminzade and McAdam 2001). Intense rejoicing would accompany victories, and despair when encountering defeats.

Some quantitative studies of participation in movements did, however, examine their impact. Positive attitudes towards the collective goods pursued in a labour union drive and in a peace demonstration in the Netherlands were shown to be very important in the motivation to participate, indeed more so than the social selective incentives involved (Klandermans 1984; Klandermans and Oegema 1987). Tarrow (1989a) empirically examined both a set of grievances and a set of demands (collective incentives) implied to be involved in Italian conflicts of the 1960s and 1970s. In the case of the Quebec independence movement, it was shown that collective goods or bads (expected cultural, status, and economic gains or losses perceived to follow independence) were extremely important factors in support of, or opposition to, that option (Pinard 1980). Moreover, in an analysis of the 1980 Quebec sovereignty referendum, an interaction between grievances and positive incentives was found; both tended to be necessary for voting support (Pinard and Hamilton 1986). Occasionally, however, aspirations were replacing grievances when, despite the absence of the latter, the incentives were perceived as positive. But in such cases support tended to be softer and very infrequent, in line with the hypothesis that it would be extremely difficult to build a strong movement on the basis of aspirations alone (256–7). Interactive effects between status and linguistic grievances and relevant incentives were also reported in subsequent studies of the same movement by Nadeau and Fleury (1995) and Mendelsohn (2003). In another series of studies of that movement rooted in a rational choice perspective, it was also found that collective costs and benefits were important, but these empirical analyses completely ignored the role of grievances (see, for instance, Blais, Martin, and Nadeau 1995; Nadeau, Martin, and Blais 1999). Finally, a study of demobilization among activists in that movement found that while grievances seemed to have been more important for their recruitment, collective incentives predominated for those who persisted in their participation (Millar and Pinard 1998).

More generally, it can be hypothesized that the ubiquitous failure of many groups, in particular those from the lower classes, to act for the redress of their grievances is not necessarily the result of their lack of resources or organization but possibly also of an emotion – their fear that *net collective bads* might be incurred if they acted.

It can also be hypothesized that since contentious collective action often opposes challengers to political authorities, reallocations of state power are then likely to be the central, when not the ultimate, incentives pursued (Wimmer, Cederman, and Min 2009).

Selective Incentives versus Moral Obligations

The arguments to be made in this section require some elaboration. In the resource mobilization and political process perspectives, one finds an emphasis not only on collective incentives, as for instance in Tilly's work, but also on selective incentives, as in Oberschall's (1973) and McCarthy and Zald's (1977) writings.

Following Olson's (1965) classic argument, mobilization in the pursuit of a collective good is seen as problematic. It should not be taken for granted that rational and self-interested members will contribute to the pursuit of a collective good, at least in large groups in which any one member's contribution will not make a perceptible difference to the group or any of its members. However much they may want that good, it is not in their interest to contribute to its provision. They should choose instead to remain *free riders*, benefiting from the collective gains obtained thanks to the contributions of others. This situation is, however, the source of a dilemma. While all members of large groups have a common interest in obtaining the collective good, all have no personal interest in paying the costs of providing it, thus remaining free riders. As a result, the collective good will not be provided. The way out of this dilemma has been the object of much debate. Olson argued that except for coercion, the provision of positive or negative selective incentives was necessary to motivate the rational members of a large group to act in a group-oriented way. Some students of social movements (Oberschall 1973; McCarthy and Zald 1977) originally accepted Olson's claim about the necessity of selective incentives, even if Oberschall convincingly argued that high levels of organization within collectivities made the provision of such incentives much easier.

There is convincing evidence, direct or implied, concerning the motivating role of selective incentives (e.g., Oberschall 1973, chaps 4–6; Pinard 1975, chap. 7; Klandermans 1984, 1997; Oliver 1984; Muller, Dietz, and Finkel 1991; Taylor 1995; Jasper 1997, 23–9; Finkel and Muller 1998; Gould 2002, 192–6; Willer 2009).[10] Of great importance are social as well as status or prestige rewards granted to group-oriented or altruistic participants making greater contributions than others. For one thing such rewards are greatly available even in resource-poor movements. Above all they carry significant consequences, as shown by Willer (2009). Such rewards lead those who receive them to make increased contributions in the future, to gain greater influence over other members, and to be more likely to generate cooperation in subsequent actions.

But many have voiced disagreements with Olson's claim about the frequency of free-riding and the necessary and sufficient character of selective incentives to resolve the dilemma. One of the strongest challenges came from Marwell and Oliver (1993, esp. chaps 4 and 8), who argued that free-riding was much less frequent than claimed by Olson and that selective incentives were neither necessary nor sufficient as a solution, although they recognized that they remained important in many situations. In their model, a dominant role is played by a "critical mass" of early contributors, defined as "a relatively small cadre of highly interested and resourceful individuals." As for free-riding, it was indeed likely to be frequent in only one form of collective action, characterized by decelerating production functions, with contributions yielding decreasing marginal returns, the highest returns being reaped with initial contributions. In this case, the critical mass, making large contributions, but with relatively high payoffs, provides the good for all. But once action reaches a basic level, additional contributions add little, leaving the others to be free riders, unless provided with selective incentives; but the ride is then cut short at the maximum. Examples of such forms of contributions mentioned by the authors are lobbying, organizational maintenance, and newsletter publication.

The propensity to free-ride is, however, reduced in an obverse form of action characterized by accelerating production functions, with increasing marginal returns from contributions, the highest returns going to later contributors. Given that early contributions by members of a critical mass produced only small increases in marginal returns, this creates a serious problem, that of overcoming the start-up costs. But members of the critical mass could be motivated to do it by the fact that their actions would set off others' actions, which would vindicate in the end their original contributions. Since late contributions would produce progressively larger returns, members of the group would stand to lose from free-riding. Examples of this given are mass actions profiting from increasing numbers of participants, such as strikes, boycotts, and collective defiance, as well as many other forms of contentious collective action. Such actions then tend to be self-reinforcing and can even become explosive. These important distinctions will be taken into consideration in our motivation theory.

The restricted role played by selective incentives was the main concern of Marwell and Oliver. Internal motives such as grievances and their emotions, aspirations, or moral obligations were, however, ignored, and expectancy of success was only implicit. Collective incentives, under the guise of "interest in the collective good," were simply assumed to be present and constituted the only other motivation factor considered, but the authors considered these subjective interests to be higher among members of the critical mass than among other participants (14–15). They were also said to be based on a wide array of factors motivating human beings, such as a desire for monetary gain, ideological commitment, solidarity, among others, but these issues were deliberately left aside (16–18). Why, however, were grievances, a basic determinant of interest in the collective good, completely ignored?

Many other authors had earlier also challenged Olson' theory, raising in particular some of those issues. While accepting Olson's dilemma, Gamson (1975, chap. 5) and Fireman and Gamson (1979) rejected the claim that selective incentives were the only solution, arguing instead that there were possible substitutes for them. More specifically, they held that individuals engaging in collective action were often drawn in by solidarity with, and loyalty to, a constituency, and/or by responsibility to principles and values. In those circumstances, they claimed, "hard" selective incentives, that is, incentives involving external positive or negative sanctions, were not required (see also Carden 1978; Oliver 1980, 1372–3).

On the whole, this claim is justified, and one can only be surprised that it should have had to be reaffirmed, given the important role traditionally assigned to ideology and social integration in the social movements literature. Yet no traces of ideology as a factor can be found in McCarthy and Zald's early work (1973, 1977), and Tilly (1978: 58) explicitly ignored it in his models. Oberschall (1973, 178ff.) did pay attention to it early, but without integrating it into his motivation scheme, although he did it later (1993, 1996).[11] Fireman and Gamson's corrective was therefore essential, and only the strong utilitarian biases of the new approach made this reaffirmation necessary.

PRINCIPLES AND IDEOLOGY

While Fireman and Gamson's arguments against Olson are theoretically important, their discussion calls for sharper distinctions. With regard to principles, Olson (1965, 64–5) commented that selfless behavior was not a solution to the free-rider problem, because making an unselfish contribution was irrational, since it would not make a perceptible difference. But he had earlier mentioned that acting on the basis of altruistic values could be rational if it provided its own moral (selective) incentives (Olson 1965, 61n). More generally, Olson returned to the problem of ideological motivation at least three times, but always to dismiss its relevance (Olson 1965, 12–13, 61n, 161 ff.).

At any rate, Olson argued that moral and ideological motives were neither sufficient nor necessary to explain rational collective action. The reasons given were, first, that they were generally a rare form of motivation and were therefore insufficient to explain that action. If even national states, sustained by the strongest ideological motives (patriotism, nationalism, communism, etc.), could not get their citizens to make voluntary contributions, neither could other large private organizations (12–13, 162). Second, they were unnecessary, since other explanations could be sufficient (61n). As for groups for which such motives were important ("mass movements," collective action by a "band of committed people" working for "lost causes"), the action was non-rational or irrational and one should turn elsewhere for a relevant theory (161–2).

Much of Olson's perspective is in this regard untenable. To be sure, one can agree that in large groups altruistic ideological motives should not be sufficient. As Lenski (1966, 30) expressed it, altruism is most likely to occur in minor events of daily life, but it is infrequent on the level of major social decisions, in which people nearly always choose their own or their group's interests over the interests of others (also Oberschall 1973, 159). If, however, altruism is rare in human affairs when large groups are involved, it is more likely to be present in contentious collective action – particularly in its radical forms – among its leaders and activists (Klandermans 1997).

As for Olson's irrationality claim, Gamson's (1975) view that the former's notion of rationality is too restricted is warranted. Because of their observations of the pervasiveness of free-riding, some selfless individuals may realize that morally it is necessary for them collectively to act "irrationally" (in Olson's terms) if a collective goal is to stand any chance of being attained. "They recognize the necessity of personal sacrifice, not in spite of, but *because* of the full force of Olson's argument" (Gamson 1975, 60; *italics* in original). Turner (1981, 14) aptly referred to this form of rationality as "exemplary rationality."

Now in addition to principles, Gamson (1975, chap. 5) and Fireman and Gamson (1979) also use notions with larger connotations, such as ideology, values, normative, and ideological appeals, as well as responsibility. Sharper distinctions need to be made. While principles such as that of communal equality are defined as a collective good, ideology also represents the articulations of one's own group's grievances – as when a worker develops a socialist ideology articulating the material grievances of his class. It could also articulate other groups' grievances – as when a white person espouses a Black civil rights ideology, thus articulating his ideal deprivations.[12] In either case, ideology, as well as principles, would be likely to greatly increase one's adherence to those causes. One could, however, particularly when one's own group is concerned, remain self-interested and not move beyond simple adherence to that ideology.

But on the basis of altruistic orientations stemming from principles, ideology, and collective identification, as well as from intense grievances, an alternative would be for one to decide to contribute to the action out of a sense of moral obligation, which would then act as another possible internal motive. It could involve a felt obligation derived from one's own moral principles or an obligation to support other group members (Van Stekeleburg and Klandermans 2007, 184). In that situation, simple adherence to principles or solidarity would not by itself lead to participation, unless one decided to act out of a sense of moral duty. It is one thing for a person to believe that some remedial corrections ought to be pursued and another to believe that she/he ought to contribute to their implementation.[13] This is where Fireman and Gamson's specific notion of responsibility is relevant and finds echo among others who have discussed the issue more specifically. While considering normative concerns as extra-rational and less important than self-interest, Hardin (1995) did hold that they remain one form of motivation in collective action. In a rational-choice model, Opp (1989, 59) included a "felt obligation to participate," but he considered it as generating its own soft selective incentive, that is, a good conscience. Hirsch (1990) elaborated a set of processes that induced participants to sacrifice their personal welfare for the group cause. Other discussions of the issue can be found in Jenkins (1983, 536–8), Snow et al. (1986, 471–2), Rule (1988, chap. 1), Jasper (1997, 134–7), and Van Stekelenburg and Klandermans (2007), and brief mentions of it have been made by Oberschall (1980, 46), Oliver (1984, 603), Turner and Killian (1987, 333), Taylor (1995, 227), and Klandermans (1997, 33, 70, 104).

Needless to say, we should expect that some emotional feelings would accompany actions motivated by felt moral obligations, particularly when those actions are highly demanding. In some way, part of such emotions are almost inherent in such obligations, since the latter are sentiments that one ought to follow the intimations of one's conscience. But feelings of pride as well as of satisfaction in doing so can be present, as will be mentioned shortly.

There is not much direct evidence concerning the impact of moral obligation on collective action participation, but there is some. This motive was spontaneously mentioned by prospective participants in Freedom Summer as a reason for their action (McAdam 1988, 45). It was also mentioned by participants in the 1985 Columbia student blockade (Hirsch 1990).

Some supporting quantitative evidence can also be found in Opp (1989), Muller and Finkel (1990), Millar and Pinard (1998), and Stürmer et al. (2003).

There is, however, much empirical quantitative and qualitative evidence concerning the strong impact of ideologically articulated grievances, material or ideal, whether in studies of the student movement (Somers 1965; Flacks 1967; Lipset 1971; Wood 1974), of the women's movement (Freeman 1973; Carden 1978; Taylor 1995), or of other contentious movements of various political persuasions (Lipset 1950; Wolfinger et al. 1964; Pinard, Kirk, and Von Eschen 1969; McEvoy III 1971; Stein 1973; Lord, Latouche, and Lacorne 1976; Low-Beer 1978; Walsh and Warland 1983; Oberschall 1993).

To be sure, as mentioned above, compliance to moral obligations normally yields its own moral selective incentive, its "intrinsic reward" (Jasper 1997, 136). However, as Gamson (1975, 58–9) and Fireman and Gamson (1979, 20–1) have argued, intrinsic rewards are of a quite different nature,[14] and they should not be equated with hard material or social incentives if one wants to keep the latter's explanatory power. Besides, the important point is that when acting under a sense of moral obligation, one is willing to incur material and social personal costs that are greater than these moral benefits (Gamson, 1975, 59; Hardin 1993).[15] As argued by Fireman and Gamson, this willingness is important for groups that have few material resources to offer as incentives.

In short, moral obligations, with their emotions, could constitute the immediate internal motives moving some actors to make selfless contributions, and to the extent that they are so moved, the collective good aimed at would constitute the necessary and sufficient external incentive underlying their action. As will be seen, moral obligations are indeed also considered as a type of internal motive in Atkinson's general motivation theory (Feather 1982a). It will be taken into account in my motivation model.[16]

SOLIDARITY AND LOYALTY

Let us now turn to Fireman and Gamson's arguments concerning solidarity and loyalty. The problem here is more complex.

Fireman and Gamson's (1979) point of departure is drawn from Stinchcombe's (1975) excellent theory of ethnic loyalty. But in that theory loyalty is fundamentally rooted in self-interest. Briefly, according to Stinchcombe the greater the degree to which individuals are integrated into an ethnic group, the greater the degree to which they have most of their life problems solved through that group and in turn the greater the degree to which their own personal fate depends on that of the group. Hence the greater their degree of loyalty to that group. But conversely that loyalty can incite its members to promote or defend the collective assets of the group, including those of its institutions and organizations. The gains or losses of the group or of any of its institutions and organizations will entail gains or losses for group members in direct relation to their degree of integration in that group. As Stinchcombe (1975, 602) puts it, a direct tie develops between a person's identity and the group, and "this direct tie is where the energy of ethnic and national loyalty comes from. An attack on such a group is an attack on a person's capacity to solve the problems of his or her life, and so it releases great patriotic energies."

But such loyalty being first and foremost self-interested, it means that the pursuit of the group's collective goods on the basis of that loyalty is rational and self-interested (see also Hardin 1995). And if so, given the proper form of action, Olson's free rider's alternative becomes a possibility, with selective incentives as a way to overcome it. Fireman and Gamson cannot therefore claim that such solidarity or loyalty, self-interested or utilitarian as it is, could be an alternative to selective incentives.

This does not mean, however, that these authors are wrong in insisting, but on different grounds, on the importance of such solidarity and loyalty in collective action. First, through that solidarity members' grievances could become much more salient and intense, something that would very substantially increase the strength of their adherence to the group's collective action. Other motivation dimensions could also be positively affected, as will be discussed in chapter 6. Second solidarity and loyalty, by strengthening adherence, could become important in the generation of a sense of moral obligation. But solidarity is only one determinant of contributions stemming from a sense of moral obligation. It is only a different avenue to such contributions, in addition to ideologies.

In short, utilitarian solidarity, certainly the most frequent type, is not a solution to the free-rider problem. It is only when such attachments lead to participation based on a sense of moral obligations that hard selective incentives become dispensable, given that free-riding is not the alternative (see Klandermans 1997, 78).

To conclude this section, one may ask whether moral obligations are the only internal motives making the provision of selective incentives unnecessary. The answer is probably negative, particularly in contentious collective action. Such incentives could be dispensed with in situations in which rational, self-interested actors falsely perceive their contributions to actions with diminishing marginal returns as making a difference. That could also occur whenever the action is dictated by very intense internal motives, such as severe threats, leading again some actors to perceive their action as crucial and making a difference. In chapter 6, the impact of collective identities and solidarity on other components of motivation will be further discussed.

Selective versus Collective Incentives

This leads us to a related point. It concerns the *necessity* not of selective but of *collective incentives,* even when actors are making self-interested contributions in line with utilitarian premises. Olson's conclusion that collective goods are insufficient in a large group to incite its members to make contributions was also challenged by Fireman and Gamson (1979), who argued that much stronger conclusions could be derived from Olson's utilitarian assumption. "If individuals are thoroughly self-interested and rational, common interests are *unnecessary* for collective action as well as insufficient – in fact, they are irrelevant ... the provision of selective incentives not only is necessary ... but is *sufficient*" (11, italics in original). Fireman and Gamson then go on to argue that surely such a generalization cannot hold, that actually actors are often "interested "in the collective good

they seek. The stronger conclusion may make sense when workers accept jobs for pay with a firm regardless of their interest in
the goods produced by that firm. But in Fireman and Gamson's
view this does not make sense in a social movement. "Whether
one's taste for chocolate affects one's propensity to take a job in
a chocolate factory, surely one's taste for civil rights affects one's
propensity to join in a civil rights movement" (14). Hence, they
conclude, if the collective good is not irrelevant for some type
of collective action, it implies that the utilitarian logic cannot be
invoked to explain it, that instead solidarity and principle are
at work.

This criticism of utilitarian logic again does not hold. Notice
first that the "chocolate" or other goods produced by business
firms are *not* collective goods but the firms' *private* ones. Hence
one need not be and one often is not "interested" in such goods
when joining a firm. On the other hand, the "civil rights" produced by a movement are obviously collective goods. It is only
for that and similar situations that the problem being raised
is relevant.

Now is that collective good necessary to motivate people to
contribute to such a movement? As implied in my previous discussion, and indeed as also argued by Fireman and Gamson,
such a collective good is not only necessary but even sufficient,
if one is entirely moved by selfless ideals and moral obligations.
But what about rational and totally self-interested actors?

Empirically, observation teaches us that even self-interested
participants needing some selective incentives to make a contribution will often have, as well, strong desires for the collective
good, so that they appear to be also motivated this way. The presence of *pure opportunists*, who by definition show no interest
in the collective good itself, creates indeed a situation in which
their motives, if admitted or perceived, are likely to be strongly
loathed by other participants. This situation is therefore likely
to be very rare, particularly in ideological movements, although
less so in populist ones. Theoretically it is obvious that Fireman
and Gamson's stronger conclusion holds in the case of the pure
opportunist: the collective good is not necessary and is indeed
irrelevant as a motivating factor, and for the pure opportunist

selective incentives are both necessary and sufficient external motives. As was seen, the role of internal motives is then likely to be played by simple aspirations, but aspirations for the selective incentives involved.

But these authors appear to assume, in the passage cited earlier, that an actor "interested" in the collective good must be motivated to engage in action by something beyond pure self-interest, that is, by solidarity or principles. This is obviously not the case. Marwell and Oliver's (1993) distinction between collective actions with accelerating production functions and those with decelerating ones is relevant in this case. In the first form of action, totally self-interested actors will be moved to action by the increasing marginal returns from the collective good, and the latter will play the same external incentive role as in the case of actors moved by moral obligations. In both cases, the internal motives involved are going to be the grievances and/or aspirations pushing them toward that good.

Conversely, if the actions involve decelerating production functions, this is more likely to involve the possibility of free-riding for totally self-seeking actors. Then Fireman and Gamson's stronger conclusion holds again, even if they do not recognize it: the collective good itself cannot motivate such actors to make a contribution. Selective incentives are again both necessary and sufficient[17] and, paradoxical as this may seem, the actor is then motivated to make a contribution in the same way as the pure opportunist. But to the extent that in those situations the collective good is unnecessary as an incentive, it follows that contributions cannot be explained by the grievances and/or aspirations pushing them toward that good. As mentioned before, the role of internal motives is then likely to be played by simple aspirations for selective incentives.

Let me add immediately that empirically these possibilities will often be combined, with actors being motivated by a mix of internal motives, grievances/emotions and/or aspirations, and moral obligations, and by collective incentives, accompanied by selective ones in actions of the decelerating type, depending on a combination of both self-interest and altruistic orientations. Great variations in the relative importance of each of these motivational components will therefore be very likely to occur. Again these specifications will become part of my model of motivation.

Incidentally, in previous chapters the frequently weak associations observed between deprivations and the emergence of collective action were discussed. The utilitarian logic tells us one additional reason for this: for the purely self-interested actor in a free-riding situation, even severe deprivations are irrelevant, at least in a direct way, to his willingness to be among the first to make a contribution.[18]

Adherence versus Resource Contribution

Let us return for a moment to the dependent variable. The apparent paradox mentioned above, as well as its practical impact, may be further lessened by the consideration of the distinction between adherents and constituents. The *adherents* or *sympathizers* are defined as those individuals and organizations that simply believe or agree with the goals of the movement, while the *constituents* or *participants* are those contributing resources for it (McCarthy and Zald 1977).[19] The reader will notice first that Fireman and Gamson's "interested" actors are simply adherents to a cause whose conversion into constituents, if it takes place, must be explained. But adherence and participation are not explained the same way. With regard to their adherence, only internal motives (grievances/emotions and/or aspirations) and collective incentives are important, given that their supportive beliefs entail no altruistic or self-interested contributions and call for no selective returns or expectancy of success. Our concern so far was with the contributions of self-interested or altruistic participants, for whom the conclusions differ.

Indeed, if the arguments developed are sound, one should observe, given mobilization efforts,[20] stronger relationships between adherence and, let us say, grievance than between participation and grievance, since in the latter case, costly moral obligations and/or selective incentives can also be involved. Interestingly enough and although no attention has been paid to such findings, it is exactly what Useem's (1980) data show: his measure of adherence to the anti-busing movement was more strongly related to deprivations than his measure of participation in anti-busing activities and groups (see his tables 3 and 5). Similarly, LeCavalier's (1983) data show that attitudinal support and potential membership in a citizens' movement were more strongly related to threats than participation and actual membership in it (compare her tables 5.2, 5.12, and 5.20).

These conclusions of course do not mean that the importance of adherents for collective action should be belittled. Quite the contrary. It is obviously much easier to convert adherents into constituents than to convert indifferents (bystander publics, in McCarthy and Zald's typology) or, for that matter, opponents. This is indeed a central point in Klandermans's (1997) theory. Once individuals agree with the goals of a movement, it becomes easier, obviously, to incite them, directly or through social networks, to make a contribution based on a mix of self-interested and disinterested motives (see also Isaac, Mutran, and Stryker 1980, 200).

Methodologically, it should be noted however that to the extent that most participants will tend to be adherents rather than pure opportunists, it will be empirically difficult to disentangle the impact of specific internal motives and of collective and/or selective incentives on their adherence and on their participation.

Motives and Perceived Incentives

Finally, a last issue must be raised. In the recent literature, there is a tendency to assume that in contentious collective action the collective goods and bads pursued are objective, well-delimited goods whose scope is perceived accurately and similarly by all those involved. This is obviously not the case. The collective goods or bads expected to flow from collective action lie, by definition, in the future, and the actors' information about them must perforce remain very imperfect, since they depend on many contingencies and since actors cannot easily assess many of these. This is certainly true when the goods imply complex social and political transformations. Actors may then be open to quite serious biases in their apprehensions of such a future. For instance, one implication of the recent findings on strike activity discussed above may be that rank and file workers are much more ill-equipped to evaluate the economic incentives of a strike than central union leaders (Smith 1979). Or, to take another example, there is in Quebec quite a range of variations in people's perceptions of the cultural and economic implications of a sovereign Quebec (see the relevant literature cited earlier).[21] This means that people will be moved not by objective collective incentives but by their own *perceptions* of them. But this poses serious problems for the mobilization process, as leaders and militants must not only raise people's consciousness regarding grievances, activate their solidarity, and sharpen their sense of moral obligation, but also convince them about the positive value of the collective goals pursued. And at times – and certainly in Quebec – the latter task appears more formidable than the former ones.

In addition to the subjective character of incentives, a strong interdependence of the various motivation components will tend to prevail,[22] not to mention the impact of participation on those components. It was already mentioned how grievances and moral obligations tend to be interrelated. Because of the prevalence of imperfect information about the incentives, their perceptions also appear to be easily affected by an individual's internal motives, following a process of cognitive consonance. The stronger one's sense of grievances/emotions, the more likely one's positive perception of the collective incentives. The two should therefore not be assumed to be independent. This is particularly the case when people are moved by a well-articulated ideology. In that case, components of that ideology, such as felt grievances, a set of ideals, the solutions proposed, and expectancy of success are all going to be highly constrained elements. Hence the importance of strong ideological beliefs in the pursuit of contentious collective action, since it insures that all motivational elements will tend to be consistent.

EXPECTANCY OF SUCCESS AS A MOTIVATIONAL COMPONENT

Atkinson's (1964) theory considers expectancy of success as a third essential motivational component of individual action. It is no less important in collective action. While it was for long neglected in the literature, its role is now increasingly recognized, not only in theories inspired by Atkinson but in others as well.

In the earlier literature on social movements, this notion was often cast in negative terms such as hopelessness, despair, and pessimism about the possibility of change, although the positive aspects of hope, faith, and a sense of efficacy were also present.[23] Blumer (1955, 199), for instance, stated early on that both dissatisfaction about some conditions and hopes for change were essential motives for social movements. Similar ideas are included in Smelser's (1963) beliefs determinant. Views about the restraining effects of hopelessness, particularly among the most destitute, were often expressed (Turner and Killian 1957, 432; 1987, 245–6; Von Eschen, Kirk, and Pinard 1969; Paige 1971; Pinard 1975; McAdam 1982). In that literature, however, this factor was not usually seen as equally indispensable as it became in Atkinson's model. But in more recent writings, the notion of expectancy of success, partly influenced by Atkinson, can be found in many models (Piven and Cloward 1979, 4; Oberschall 1980; Klandermans 1984, 1997; Opp 1988, 1989; Oliver 1989; Hirsch 1990; Muller, Dietz, and Finkel 1991, Finkel and Muller 1998). This notion also appears under the guise of agency, or the consciousness of political efficacy, in Gamson (1992a), as well as in Van Zomeren et al. (2004), Klandermans (1997), and Klandermans, Van der Toorn, and Van Stekelenburg (2008).

Expectancy of success can focus on various angles of an episode of collective action. It can be related to the mobilization process (e.g., securing enough material or human resources), to the effectiveness of various tactics and strategies (peaceful or violent, radical or moderate, direct action or the electoral route, sit-ins or site occupations, etc.), to the ultimate goals pursued (to be totally or partially attained), as well as to intermediate and

partial goals (e.g., success of a demonstration) or to the ability
to provide sufficient selective incentives and to escape selective
costs. In particular, expectancy of success in immediate, specific,
local actions may be more important to motivating participants than if it is related to any long-term, national strategies
(Oberschall 1980; McAdam 1988, 217). In Klandermans's book
(1997, 80), expectancy of success must be related to three action
components, that is, expectations that one's participation will
contribute to the success of the action, that the action will succeed if enough people participate, and that enough other people
will actually participate. The importance of the various aspects
mentioned is likely to vary between leaders and ordinary participants, and in general the greater the costs and risks of the
action, the more important expectancy of success is likely to be
as a motivating factor, and conversely when costs are minimal
(ibid., 81; Pinard and Hamilton 1986). The strength of the internal motives and external incentives involved will also make such
expectation less crucial.

Expectancy of success can be amplified by relevant emotions.
As in the case of moral obligations, such emotions are almost
inherent in such expectations. Hopes, enthusiasm, feelings of
self-confidence, and even political efficacy have all been suggested as playing that role. Conversely, emotions such as despair,
cynicism, and resignation would tend to dampen any perceived
possibility of change (Jasper 1998, 406; Aminzade and McAdam
2001, 31, 45; Taylor 2010, 125).

The development of expectancy of success depends on many
factors. In addition to the presence of a general sense of political efficacy, it could depend on the development of new political opportunities (such as divisions within the elites, new
governments more favourable to challengers, new supporting
allies, political instabilities) (Tarrow 1998), but also on social
changes and socioeconomic progress that increased the group's
self-confidence (McAdam 1982; Pinard 1997a), the relative
power balance of the contending groups, past successes in recent
encounters, and the authorities' and other groups' sympathies
and tolerance towards dissidents. In general all intermediate

and partial successes will greatly reinforce the expectations of future success.

SUMMARY

In this chapter, the often ambiguous impact attributed to aspirations, a second internal motive, was considered, leading us to reassess the confusing assertions found among various authors and to distinguish in particular the different impact of that motive among leaders and followers. In particular, the frequent assertions that in contentious politics movement leaders are solely motivated by their aspirations for collective goods, especially those potentially accruing to their group, and by selective incentives was definitely rejected. Aspirations alone cannot indeed easily move collectivities to engage in widespread contention. A third internal motive, moral obligation, also had to be introduced. It was argued that this motive ought to be disentangled from sweeping generalizations concerning principles, ideology, and solidarity, in order in particular to distinguish the sacrifices endured because of one's sense of duty from the self-interests pursued out of, say, solidarity.

Moving to external incentives, a basic proposition held that both internal motives and external incentives were necessary to motivate one to engage in contentious action. This proposition, part of motivation theory, has rarely retained the attention of researchers; but the few times it was tested, support for it was confirmed.

Critics of Olson argued that selective incentives were not the necessary element he claimed them to be. In forms of action characterized by accelerating production functions – that is, the most frequent forms in contentious action – these incentives were not necessary, since late contributions produce progressively larger returns and since members of the group would stand to lose from free-riding.

Finally, expectancy of success was introduced as the last major component of motivation, although its central importance is all too often not recognized, being only mentioned in passing. Its relevance bears not only on the ultimate goals of movements but also, among other things, on intermediate ones, on the ability to secure resources and allocate them profitably and on the various tactics and strategies selected.

Now that all these components and sub-components of motivation have been delineated, the next task is to present my model of motivation and to indicate the variations in motivation likely to be observed in different groups in different contexts.

5

A Model of Motivation in Contentious Collective Action

The many theoretical issues discussed in previous chapters have opened the way for the statement of a comprehensive model of motivation. It offers a synthetic reconciliation of the implicit and explicit, but partial, theories of motivation prevailing in divergent approaches to contentious action, while also integrating elements ignored by them.[1] As already mentioned, Atkinson's (1964, chap. 9; also Feather 1982a) psychological theory of achievement motivation constitutes the point of departure. But since it bears on the action of individuals engaged in the pursuit of private goods, an elaboration of it is necessary to deal with the pursuit of collective goods, especially in contentious collective action. Atkinson's model already inspired Korpi's (1974) power balance model of collective conflict, which brought together elements of the relative deprivation and of the resource mobilization approaches, although Korpi's model involved a more straightforward application of Atkinson's model than ours.[2] In turn, Muller (1979) developed a model based on Atkinson's and Korpi's, to which he added normative beliefs about the justification of the action. But like Korpi, Muller disregarded alternative solutions to Olson's dilemma.[3]

Following Atkinson, I hold that to be motivated to participate in contentious collective action, an actor must be moved at the same time by *internal motives*, which are the internal states, needs, forces, or drives *pushing* the actor to action, *and* by *external incentives*, which represent the goods "out there" *pulling* the actor into action, *and* by *expectancy of success*. The *utility* or *value* of the action is a multiplicative function of motives and incentives. Notice that the model is a *multiplicative* one, with these three major components all necessary for an action to take place.[4] The model is of course about actual participation. A consideration of simple adherence to a cause, without contribution, will involve modifications to be examined subsequently.

With regard to invidual participation, Atkinson considered only one internal motive, a motive to achieve. That motive was viewed as a general and stable disposition of the person, such as need achievement, although at times the motive could be a situational characteristic, not general or stable, such as hunger (Atkinson and Feather 1966). In Korpi (1974) and in Muller's 1979 paper, as in our model, the motives considered are not necessarily stable, but while a single internal motive, relative deprivation, prevailed in these authors' theories, there is more than one in ours.

On the basis of earlier discussions, it is postulated, first, that all kinds of shared deprivations or felt grievances, actual or potential (threats), absolute or relative, material or ideal, relevant or displaced, hard or soft, can theoretically play that role,[5] this together with relevant action-oriented emotions such as anger, indignation, or fears. However, simple material deprivations and ideologically articulated material and ideal deprivations, whether actual or potential (threats), absolute or relative, are likely to be the essential ones. Above all, for most actors the important deprivations are going to be *relevant* grievances rather than simply displaced but real grievances,[6] or displaced generalized tensions or anxieties – that is, relevant grievances that dictate the framing of problems and solutions shared by members of an acting group through collective identification.[7] With regard to emotions, those accompanying grievances are presumed to exert the strongest effects and are therefore explicitly mentioned jointly with grievances as one internal motive.

Second, while the presence of some internal motives is necessary, grievances/emotions are only one type of them, and they could come in combination with, or may even be replaced by another type, simple aspirations. Although generally less important than grievances, aspirations ought to belong in a comprehensive model. For one thing, they are the most likely motive involved, as argued before, in the pursuit of selective incentives. They could also be a dominant motive in the pursuit of particular collective goods by leaders of challenging collectivities. In contrast, with regard to the general collective goods pursued by challenging actors, the predominant drives among ordinary participants are likely to be shared grievances, while among their leaders, shared aspirations could possibly accompany grievances, but most often as secondary motives.

Third, aspirations are no more necessary than grievances/emotions. As internal motives, any of them or both could come in combination with, or, more rarely, be replaced by, feelings of moral obligations rooted in norms, values, and ideologies, and dictating selfless contributions to collective action.[8] Their role would tend to increase with increasing personal costs of the action, as in risky situations or among leaders generally. Notice that Feather (1982a, 87; 1990), a collaborator of Atkinson, argued that both needs and values should be taken into account, as different internal motives, with values involving "normative considerations of 'oughtness' and desirability." In short, singly or in combinations, grievances/emotions, aspirations, and moral obligations could be the internal motives involved; but at least one of them must be present.

In addition to the internal motives, there must be some *pulls* provided by perceived *external incentives*. Now one might think that the collective goods pursued would be the only external incentive involved. As was argued, the situation is, however, more complex. There are three possibilities, one for altruistic contributors and two for self-interested ones.

Altruistic actors moved solely by a sense of moral obligation are not of course recruited by selective incentives. They are simply moved by a sense of duty to pursue the attainment of some *collective incentives*.

In the case of a contributor moved solely by self-interest, general or particular collective incentives are also the main incentives involved in situations in which the benefits that that contributor derives from the provision of that good exceed her or his contributing costs. An example of this, as discussed before, would be contributors in mass actions with accelerating production functions whose participation would make a differ- ence – or who perceive it as making such a difference – in terms of increasing marginal returns on the collective goods (Marwell and Oliver 1993).

Finally, for wholly self-interested contributors considering it to their advantage to free ride, as in actions with decelerating production functions, the only necessary incentives to partici- pate are some *selective incentives* overriding their personal costs. Indeed, even when these members are highly interested in the collective good, selective incentives, paradoxically, will be both the necessary and the sufficient ones to account for their action. This would hold *a fortiori* for pure opportunists, if any, who are not in the first place interested in the collective good, but only in selective rewards.

As argued before, however, most of the time actors will be motivated by a mix of grievances/emotions and/or aspirations and/or moral obligations, with these components prevailing in various proportions. If so, both collective and selective incen- tives will be necessary for one to make a contribution. In par- ticular, and except among pure opportunists, most of the time aspirations for selective incentives are not going to be strong enough to motivate a contributor, and a sense of moral obliga- tion to pursue a highly valued collective good, even if secondary, will often be involved.

Finally, collective action will not take place unless acting members of the group feel at least some expectancy of success. This is a simple, but also a necessary, motivational component. The lack of any expectancy of success, more than any other mobilization problem, has no doubt been immediately respon- sible for the failure to act of innumerable groups throughout human history, groups that otherwise had the proper configura- tions of internal motives and external incentives. This is, there- fore, with the free rider problem, another motivational hurdle faced by social movements. As mentioned before, the problem is particularly serious among groups affected by severe and long- endured deprivations. A motivation model ought therefore, following Atkinson, to consider expectancy of success as a very significant factor.

Expectancy of success about the various angles of the action mentioned could easily differ; for instance, there could be strong, positive expectations regarding the effects of immediate, local tactics of a movement but weak or even negative ones regarding the attainment of its overall goals, or vice-versa. However, some positive expectations about at least some angles of the action will be needed to lead one to participate.

Besides grievances to which emotions should be explicitly tied, it is not believed to be essential to do so for the other components.[9] For one thing, selective incentives are rarely accompanied by significant emotions, except occasionally for social incentives. With regard to the other components, emotions, while undoubtedly present, can be presumed to play a less significant role, as in the case of collective incentives, and they are at any rate almost inherent in some of them, as in expectancy of success and even feelings of moral obligation. Only, therefore, implicit considerations of their presence and impact appear to be needed in the model; but they could always be explicitly introduced in any analysis, as is done with grievances.

The foregoing separate examination of each component of motivation needs to be summarized systematically by showing how all the components combine to account in multiplicative relationships for the participation of various types of contributors in various forms of action, as well as for simple adherence to a cause.

THE MODEL

With regard to participation, the actor who is solely self-interested and who participates in contentious actions with a decelerating production function, the probability of free-riding will be high. To participate, therefore, this actor will require selective incentives and her/his degree of participation, P_{id}, should be determined according to the following equation:

$$P_{id} = A_s \times S \times T_s. \tag{1a}$$

Motivation is then produced by A_s, the degree of aspiration for selective incentives, times S, the net positive attraction of these selective rewards, times T_s, the expectancy of obtaining them. Let me add that this formula should be valid, whether the actor is a pure opportunist, for whom the goal pursued is irrelevant, or a purely self-interested actor but one who cares about the collective good.

If the solely self-interested participant is engaging, as initiator or follower, in some action with an accelerating production function, free riding and selective incentives, as was seen, are not a problem, since the actor would be engaging in action for greater collective gains, and the participation, P_{ia}, should be accounted for by the following formula:

$$P_{ia} = (GE + A_c) \times C \times T_c. \tag{1b}$$

Motivation in that case results from GE, the degree of relevant grievances/emotions, plus A_c, the degree of simple aspiration for the collective goods (with GE likely to be much more important than A_c), times C, the net value of those goods, times T_c, the expectancy of success in getting them. In the decelerative case, this type of motivation could also partially account for the participation of members of the critical mass, who by definition show "high interest" in the cause; in their case, strongly felt grievances/emotions, particularly ideal ones, and strongly attractive collective goods should be important motivating forces.

Conversely, if the actor's participation rests solely on altruistic orientations, her/his participation, P_a, should be accounted for by the following formula:

$$P_a = O \times C \times T_c. \tag{2}$$

In that situation, the actor's motivation will be determined by O, the strength of his/her feeling of moral obligation, times C, times T_c. This could be quite important among those making substantial contributions, such as members of the critical mass, particularly in the accelerative mode, when early payoffs are relatively small. Notice that while grievances/emotions do not appear directly in equation (2), they exert very strong indirect effects as a major determinant of an actor's sense of moral obligation.

In most empirical situations, a mix of motivational determinants is likely to prevail. Most of the time participants will be moved by both self-interest and altruism – the first being often more important – so that equations (1a) or (1b) will combine additively with (2) into P_1 or P_2 as overall degrees of participation:[10]

$$P_1 = (A_s \times S \times T_s) + (O \times C \times T_c) \text{ or} \qquad (3a)$$
$$P_2 = ([GE + A_c] \times C \times T_c) + (O \times C \times T_c). \qquad (3b)$$

Turning to simple adherence, rather than participation, the motivation model is greatly simplified, since adherence does not rest on a sense of moral duty to act and calls for no selective incentives or expectancy of success and since therefore different forms of action need not be taken into consideration. A person's adherence H will be motivated only by a mix of grievances/emotions (mostly based on material or ideal deprivations) and aspirations (with again the first likely to be more important), times the net value of the collective incentive, that is,

$$H = (GE + A_c) \times C. \qquad (4)$$

While this model is very different from most others, it bears greater similarity to Klandermans' (1997) early models.[11] Differences remain, however, since Klandermans (1984, 584; 1997, 26) appeaed to rely on an expectancy-value approach different from that of Atkinson. While grievances were an important factor in his model of adherence, the collective goods pursued were not seriously considered in that model. Conversely, in his model of participation proper, the role of internal motives and especially that of grievances were no longer explicit; it stressed mainly the role of collective and selective incentives, as well as other solutions to Olson's dilemma. While the utility or value of the action in Atkinson's model involved the interaction of internal motives and external incentives, that value in Klandermans takes into account only the collective incentives. Put differently, adherence and participation are considered as a motivation sequence rather than as two separate motivational phenomenons. The view adopted here is that when an actor decides to participate, all three motivational components are necessarily involved. This is particularly so since the level of grievances/emotions will probably need to be higher for participation than for simple adherence. Klandermans' participation model remains too close to the perspectives of the current structural approaches, which ignore the role of internal motives. Moreover, his participation model disregards the role of aspirations and, more importantly, the role of moral obligation and their interrelations with other motivational components. Given that these motives are neither general nor stable, they should be considered when working within Atkinson's approach.

In more recent papers, Klandermans and his coauthors (Klandermans 2004; Van Stekelenburg and Klandermans 2007; Klandermans, Van der Toorn, and Van Stekelenburg 2008) presented modified, but somewhat different, motivational frameworks. In the last paper, the authors' framework covers four elements: grievances, efficacy, collective identity, and emotions (anger).[12] Moral obligations and incentives, in particular, are not included, although they appear in the 2007 version of the framework, in which obligations are derived from identity and ideology, and incentives are part of the instrumentality cluster. No interactions are hypothesized in those papers.

OTHER VARIATIONS IN MOTIVATIONAL PATTERNS

In addition to the major variations in motivation according to the self-interest/altruism alternatives and according to decelerative/accelerative forms of action, other variations are likely to be substantial. While some of them may have been mentioned before, it may be useful to regroup all of them according to the types of participants involved, the types of social movements or collective action considered, the phases of the actor's participation, and the stages of the collective action itself. Unfortunately, there is not much research that substantiates such differences, so that the discussion will perforce remain tentative.

Types of Participants

With regard to the types of participants involved, a first key hypothesis is that there will be of course much variation in the motivation of challengers and that of their opponents. While actual grievances will tend to be important among the first, feelings of threats to the valued resources they control and to their power are likely to be crucial among those in positions of authority. Material selective incentives may also be scarce among challengers, but social ones important. Both could be partly compensated by a sense of moral obligation, while ample material rewards inherent in their positions will play an important role for their opponents, as well as strong fears of failure to retain all their advantages.

A second general hypothesis, as partly discussed before, would concern the possibility of differences within the challenging group between rank and file participants and militants or leaders, in particular those of the critical mass. In actions of the accelerating type, material grievances, especially economic ones, and their emotions should tend to predominate as internal motives among participating followers, particularly those from lower social strata, with the net value of the collective goods envisioned and the expectancy of success in getting them involved as other components, all this according to equation (1b), applying to interested contributors expecting greater collective gains. The pattern of equation (1a), covering self-interested actors requiring selective incentives, would apply in fewer cases among ordinary members, since possibly they would be less likely to participate in actions of the decelerative kind leading to free-riding or selective incentives.

Conversely, the same equation (1a) would be more relevant among organizers, leaders, and activists, and to a lesser extent among other participants from higher social strata, for whom selective incentives would be relevant. But these leaders would also be very likely to be moved, as in the accelerating case, by material grievances, with status and political deprivations playing a greater role, but also by ideal deprivations.[13] Aspirations for greater general – at times particular – collective goods and/

or feelings of moral obligation could also be more important internal motives among them, with equation (1b) as well as (2) – the latter for the altruistic case – being the relevant ones. The patterns just discussed for leaders would also tend to prevail among all conscience constituents,[14] but equation (2) might be more important among them. As mentioned before, equation (1b), involving the expectation of greater collective gains, might well apply to the critical mass in either forms of action. Finally, let me add that under (1b), among rank and file members, the impact of grievances/emotions, compared to that of collective incentives, would be more important, while the reverse would tend to prevail among organizers and leaders.[15] Moreover, with regard to the expectancy of success, leaders might be influenced more by long-term and ultimate goal expectations, while followers would be more likely to respond to the possibility of immediate and partial successes.

There are not many studies with distinct analyses of the motivations of members and leaders, and there are none bearing on the detailed arguments just developed, but the available ones support our general hypotheses (Lipset 1950; Rule and Tilly 1975, 66; LeCavalier 1983; compare also with Stein 1973 and Pinard 1975, bearing on the leaders and followers of the populist Social Credit movement in Quebec).

Another basic difference among participants concerns the types of contributions requested. Occasional or once-only participants would differ in their motivation from lasting participants, whether part-time or full-time. So would participants exposed to low- or high-cost or risk activities (see Klandermans 1997, 89–92). The differences in motivation would again be along the same lines as those just discussed for members and leaders. Selective incentives, in particular, could be very relevant among organizers and leaders engaged in intense, lasting, and/ or high-risk activity. Finally expectancy of success is likely to increase with the intensity of one's participation (Passy 2001).

Types of Movements and Contentious Action

Motivations are likely to vary between types of movements and of contentious action. Considering the second first, collective actions of the defensive type, in particular in responses to threats or to suddenly imposed grievances (e.g., in a nuclear accident), as opposed to other forms of protest, pertain to the accelerative mode and are therefore most likely to be motivated, as in equation (1b), by strongly felt grievances/emotions, and attractive collective solutions and the expectancy of reaching them.

Social movements could be distinguished along a protest-reform dimension, whereas protest movements are characterized by limited policy goals, and reform movements by goals for large-scale social rearrangements. One would expect ideology to play a much larger role and selfless commitments to be more prevalent in the latter, while in protest movements, particularly of lower-class and economically marginal groups, economic deprivations would play a major role (see Snow, Soule, and Cress 2005, 1203, about homeless protest), and selective incentives might be important among their leaders. Analogous distinctions would prevail, respectively, between movements choosing the electoral route and movements opting for nonroutine forms of contention.

Another way to look at that is to compare in the Western world the old working class, farmers, and other populist movements of the 1930s with the so-called new social movements of the 1960s and beyond, the latter including communal movements of American Blacks, students, women, gays and lesbians, ethnoregional and religious groups, as well as single-issue movements bearing on ecology, peace and nuclear weapons, and pro-choice or pro-life issues. Again, the hypothesis regarding participants from lower social strata would be most relevant for movements of the 1930s, since they would tend to rely heavily on the widespread mobilization of their beneficiary base. Conversely, post-1960s movements would most likely be disproportionately based on sections of the middle class, especially professionals and intellectuals (Pinard and Hamilton 1984, 1989), and to manifest a lower degree of inter-class mobilization. Hence the motivations attributed to higher-class participants above are here again highly relevant.

More generally, differences in motivational patterns should be observed between ethnoregional communal movements in which the communal groups are characterized by both high degrees of segmentation or self-enclosure, with minimal ties to other groups, and high degrees of internal organization, with strong traditional or associative ties within the group, as opposed to movements of other communal groups, such as women, or any protest action of other collectivities, in which such segmentation and/or internal organization are weaker or absent. According to Oberschall (1973, chap. 4), who assumes grievances (implicitly constant) in all cases, the first are not only much more prone to rapid and enduring mobilization but also conducive to bloc mobilization, that is, mobilization of blocs of highly organized and socially involved people as opposed to the recruitment of solitary individuals. It can easily be hypothesized that segmentation and internal organization in the first type of movements should greatly facilitate the development of stronger senses of grievances and emotions, and of opposition to those responsible for them. The senses of grievances would also tend to be more enduring and, if in abeyance during some periods, they could easily be reactivated by mobilization efforts and regain a high degree of salience. In addition, such a social structure, by making its members strongly dependent on the group (Stinchcombe 1975), could provide powerful selective incentives when needed and much reduced personal costs. This is the main motivational component considered by Oberschall in this situation, under the guise of low risk/reward ratios. Concretely it means strong social support for participation, strong sanctions against non-participation, and reduced sanctions by non-participants against participation. Bloc mobilization could also reduce the individual costs of participation by making individuals join as groups. Among leaders, individual rewards would be closely tied to the group's collective demands. Indeed, the salience of collective goods would be high among all members of communal groups, given their strong dependence on the group. Finally, expectancy of success would be less likely to be weakened by exposure to opponents' counter arguments.

Conversely, all these motivation effects would be weaker in social movements of collectivities with weaker segmentation and/or internal organization. In particular, new grievances/

emotions, as in some single-issue movements (e.g. ecology, pro-choice), could remain unarticulated for longer periods and require more framing and mobilization before generating strong motives.[16] In addition, middle-class members of subordinate communal groups are likely to be particularly sensitive to status and political grievances, while their lower-class members could be more sensitive to communal economic differentials (Pinard and Hamilton 1986). Within the middle class, intellectuals in communal movements would tend to be the most sensitive to all the grievances already mentioned, as well as to cultural ones (Pinard forthcoming).

With regard to movements of ethnoregional groups seeking political decentralization or independence, motivations among members of richer regions are likely to differ from those of members of poorer/subordinate ones. The motivations of the first would rest on fewer grievances but on strong positive economic returns as collective incentives, while the second would be driven by stronger deprivations and weaker, if not negative, economic incentives. The situation is analogous for industrial conflicts during good versus bad economic periods, as discussed previously. In the first case, workers going on strike possibly face weaker economic deprivations but the strong positive incentives of favourable labor markets conditions, while the reverse holds for the rarer strikes occurring in bad times. In his study of Italian protest during the late 1960s and early 1970s, Tarrow (1989a, 119–22) also compared strike events with all other less institutionalized protest events and found the former more likely to be associated with demands for new rights and benefits, while the second were more likely to center on demands for the redress of grievances.

It might be mentioned that coups d'état at times represent ideal types of collective action by segments of the elites, especially the military, in pursuit of their aspirations for collective power, although at times leaders of such coups could also have developed grievances against the ruling elites. Finally, collective actions spurred by extreme political disabilities, such as political exclusion, are likely to be explosive and violent, as exemplified in civil wars, discussed in chapters 2 and 4.

Phases of Participation

Modifications in motivation could prevail according to the phases of people's participation. Snow and his colleagues (1986) have insisted that willingness to participate is not a static but rather a processual, even stage-like phenomenon that it is continually reassessed, and that frame alignment in its various types is essential for the analysis of such a process. Framing results, both before and during various phases of participation, include an increase in felt grievances, emotions, and moral obligations, the growing salience of and attraction to the collective good as a solution, and an increased sense of efficacy, including the amplification, extension, and transformation of these dispositions. The motivation to participate is thereby greatly increased and, during demobilization phases, its decrease is likely to be less pronounced. We will come back to the role of framing in more detail in chapter 6. Another phase variation observed is that while grievances were the main determinant for joining a movement, continued participation appeared to rest more on collective incentives (Millar and Pinard 1998). It was also suggested that while grievances played a critical mobilization role in the early phases of recruitment, structural factors became more important once action got under way (Gurr 1993b, 189).

Other changes through time concern, first, the likely under-evaluations of the personal costs of participation among new recruits and the subsequent more accurate assessment of these costs as time goes on. Or, second, the actual costs of participation at the beginning might be relatively small, but yielding to demands for increased participation might raise with time these costs substantially. These situations could lead to withdrawal or to resistance to such demands unless a greater sense of moral duty developed and/or increases occurred in social sanctions against withdrawal, as well as in positive selective incentives for continued participation. Successes in various forms of participation may also turn out to run short of expectations, reducing commitment in all the motivation alternatives of our model (Klandermans 1997, 30ff.). Conversely, partial successes toward reaching the goals pursued may reduce the strength of one's felt grievances and of one's sense of duty and thus decrease the attraction of the ultimate goal.

Phases of Movements and Contentious Actions

Finally, some motivational components will vary according to the phases of development of movements and collective actions. First, in his diffusion model of loosely structured collective action, Oberschall (1980) argued, contrary to what was just written, that any action that meets with midway success will increase further the expectancy of future success among participants and, in particular, will stimulate that expectancy among adherents or bystanders not yet converted into participants. This could lead to increased mobilization and collective action, with in turn the possibility of repeated cycles of success and growth. With movements gaining momentum, risk/reward ratios would tend to decrease – lower risks and /or higher rewards – facilitating further the recruitment of additional participants (Oberschall 1973, 163). With an adequate communication of these processes, diffusion of the action could occur, leading to its clustering in time and space.

Conversely, failures or defeats in the attainment of any short-term or long-term goal would likely give rise to opposite cycles of reduced expectancy of success, demobilization among most supporters, and contraction in the scope of the action. Such processes, for instance, occurred on a large scale in the Quebec independence movement as a consequence of its defeats in the referendums on sovereignty of 1980 and 1995 (Pinard 1997a). But among small groups of highly militant activists, failures or slow progress could on the contrary strengthen the determination to act through more radical forms of action, as in the American Black Power movement.

Failures and defeats are not the only outcomes that could put an end to cycles of intermediate successes and growth. Victories in reaching some ultimate goals could have the same effects, as happened when the American women's rights movement won the suffrage in 1920. The decline that followed did not however lead to the disappearance of the movement and its reconstruction from scratch during the 1950s. Instead, argues Taylor (1989), the movement went into a phase of abeyance, during which smaller groups of highly committed activists maintained a reduced movement that was alive for a few decades until new circumstances and renewed purposes could lead to its resurgence. While Taylor examines many factors allowing the movement to survive in abeyance, the one dealing with the motivations of the activists is relevant to this discussion. Without any expectancy of immediate success, what became the dominant motive was, it is suggested, a strong sense of moral obligation rooted in intense levels of commitment to the movement ideology and the willingness of the surviving volunteers to endure sacrifices of time, energy, and financial resources. Conversely, however, strong personal ties of love and friendship were positive social incentives providing an additional source of motivation to maintain the movement alive (766–7).

Another important source of changes in motivation during the phases of development of movements is the emergence of new or expanding political opportunities or their contraction. Political opportunities, now one of the most popular concepts in structural approaches, are "consistent signals to social or political actors which either encourage or discourage them to use their internal resources to form social movements." Among the encouraging signals, the most salient ones include the opening up of access to power, changing or unstable political alignments, the appearance of influential allies, and conflicts within and among elites (Tarrow 1996, 54). Analyses of their positive impact on movement dynamics were mostly centered on the emergence and development of collective action, more rarely on their intermediate effect on one motivational component, that is, an increase in the expectancy of success, an effect that can be very substantial indeed. But this was generally at least implicity recognized and explicitly discussed by some authors. McAdam wrote that subjectively challengers experience shifting political opportunities as events "communicating much about their prospects for successful collective action," all this contributing to their cognitive liberation through which unjust situations are seen as "subject to change" (McAdam 1982, 48, 51). Tarrow even defined opportunities earlier as factors leading "people to undertake collective action by affecting their expectations for success or failure" (Tarrow 1994, 85; see also Klandermans 1997, chap. 7). Another positive impact of opportunities, this one on collective incentives, is that they increase the power of insurgent groups and thus encourage their mobilization by lowering the risks of participation (McAdam 1982, 43).

But there is another side to the impact of political opportunities. Like failure, as mentioned before, tightening opportunities have been observed not to dampen collective action but to further stimulate it by intensifying and amplifying emotions of anger and indignation. This is what Gould (2004) observed among lesbians and gay men who engaged in more militant activism as a result of an "outrageous" US Supreme Court decision restricting their rights. But note that in this case tightening opportunities were the result of actions by judicial authorities, not of structural changes; this made them more repulsive.

Briefly, somewhat analogous remarks can be made about the effects of repression or facilitation. Repression by authorities could greatly increase the costs of mobilization and action, both collectively and individually, by disrupting organization, freezing resources, increasing penalties and risks, and thus reducing mobilization and action possibilities, with the reverse holding in the case of facilitation (Tilly 1978). All this would also imply in repressive situations a significant decline in expectancies of success but in all likelihood a substantial intensification in the levels of grievances and emotions, with new ones produced by repression piling up over the initial ones, and in the strength of collective identities (Gurr 1993a).

CONCLUSION

Before reaching final conclusions, I want to turn briefly in a final chapter to two crucial social-psychological dimensions affecting motivation itself. Motivational factors affect not only contentious collective action; they are themselves fashioned by dynamic framing activities and collective identities that constantly reconstruct these factors.

6

Important Factors Affecting Motivation

So far the central concern has been with a detailed examination of potential motivational dimensions and of their impact on support of and participation in social movements. This analysis represented in many respects a static perspective. To be sure considerations of more dynamic aspects were presented in the last two sections of the previous chapter, aspects bearing on changes in motivation according to the phases of members' participation and the phases of movement development. Successes or failures, political opportunities, and repression or facilitation were claimed to alter grievances and selective costs and rewards. But more can be said about general factors bringing about such changes in motivational dimensions when the latter are seen as dependent rather than independent variables. In this chapter, two important cultural factors that can be assumed to be among those exerting the strongest impact on motivation will be examined. First, the effects of framing processes, only briefly mentioned before, will be examined, given their very close relation to motivation. Then the role of collective identities, the object of increasing attention in the literature will be considered; the fact that many consider them as motivating factors is alone a good reason to assess their role.

FRAMING PROCESSES AND MOTIVATION

The study of framing processes, as collective processes of interpretation, attribution, and social construction, represented a rejuvenation of earlier concerns with the impact of beliefs and ideology in social movements. Framing processes have even come to be seen, together with political opportunites and mobilizing structures, as one of the three central and interrelated sets of factors in the analysis of social movements (McAdam, McCarthy, and Zald 1996). The impact of framing processes on motivation and its modifications will be examined and will be seen as particularly direct, given that many of the processes of framing construction bear on motivational components. In the review of the framing perspective in the first chapter, it was seen that grievances were a central element of collective action frames. But frames play a major role for other motivational components as well.

David Snow and his collaborators have been the main instigators of the framing perspective. Their collective action frames are defined as "action-oriented sets of beliefs and meanings that inspire and legitimate the activities and campaigns of a social movement organization (SMO)." Frames interpret and assign meaning to events and conditions, simplifying and condensing them in ways that can instigate action (Benford and Snow 2000, 614). This is reached through frame alignment processes, referring "to the linkage of individual and SMO interpretive orientations, such that some set of individual interests, values, and beliefs, and SMO activities, goals, and ideology are congruent and complementary" (Snow et al. 1986, 464). "Framing is a dynamic, ongoing process," and frames are "continuously being constituted, contested, reproduced, transformed, and/or replaced during the course of social movement activity" (Benford and Snow 2000, 628). Such a process implies continuous social interactions between rank and file participants, activists, and leaders (Klandermans 1997, 45–52).

According to that perspective, there are three core framing tasks involved, as briefly mentioned before. The first, diagnostic framing, concerns the identification of a problem – of an unjust situation – and the attribution of blame for that situation to a responsible agent. The second task, prognostic framing, involves the articulation of a proposed solution to the problem and the identification of appropriate strategies for remedial action. The final task, motivational framing, constitutes a call to action, given that the first two alone, while creating a consensus, may not produce corrective action. It considers the motives that should incite an adherent to get involved in action (Snow and Benford 1988; Benford and Snow 2000, influenced in this by Klandermans 1997).

Along somewhat different lines Gamson's (1992a) collective action frame also involves three components, only the first of which is the same as that of Snow and his colleagues. Gamson's components are injustice, accompanied by emotions such as anger and moral indignation against those responsible for it; agency, as a consciousness of political efficacy in changing these conditions; and collective identity, the definition of a "we" and an adversarial "they."

The reader will notice that these collective action frames assume models of motivation that involve components close to some in my model. In Gamson's view, the first two components, felt injustice and agency, correspond to two important motivational dimensions in my model, grievances/emotions and expectancy of success. Similarly, in the framing perspective of Snow and his collaborators, two of the components, injustices in the diagnostic frame and solutions in the prognostic one, correspond to the grievances and, this time, collective incentives in my model. On the other hand, the identity component in Gamson, as argued before and in greater detail in the next section, should be kept analytically separate. But neither of these frames consider systematically all motivational components of the model presented.

A second important contribution in the work of Snow and his collaborators is the elaboration of four strategic alignment processes, some of which are central to motivational dynamics. These processes are, first, frame bridging, the linking of unconnected but ideologically congruent frames bearing on an issue or a problem, this possibly occurring between a movement and individuals; second, frame amplification, the idealization, embellishment, clarification, or invigoration of existing values and beliefs; third, frame extension, the extension of an SMO primary frame to include other issues and concerns presumed important to some potential adherents; and fourth, frame transformation, changing old understandings and meanings and/or generating new ones (Snow et al. 1986; Benford and Snow 2000).

The implications of that analysis are that the framing of the motivational components of my model must first be developed and articulated within the movement leadership and/or within a person's social networks, aligning possibly divergent and contested perspectives in their midst, and that they must be proposed and aligned with the perspective, possibly already present, albeit weakly articulated, of potential adherents or even actual members, all of this in a dynamic process of continual changes. Concerning motivation, what is important is that framing will constantly articulate or modify, but mostly reinforce, the strength of the various motivational components, thus making them more likely to increase a person's propensity to engage in action. The various framing tasks and frame alignment processes concerning the motivational components will be considered in turn.

First, the diagnostic and prognostic framings of all groups must become congruent and complementary. Thus, among potential recruits the first major task is the transformation of objective deprivation into felt grievances and appropriate emotions. This may be done almost automatically in some cases, as with suddenly imposed grievances, or individuals may themselves first develop feelings of dissatisfaction toward some situation, but the process could often involve more complex framing work for most forms of contention. In particular, situations taken for granted or seen as normative or acceptable must first be reframed as objective deprivations and then reframed as unjust, immoral, or degrading, and in need of change (Snow et al. 1986, 474–5). Even when conditions are perceived as grievances by sympathetic adherents, serious or mild feelings of resignation would have to be transformed into more action-oriented emotions, such as righteous anger and indignation or fear. But all in all congruence in the definition of grievances and emotions may often not be too problematic, and consensus in this regard may be reached more easily than in the case of other motives.

Within prognostic framing, the attainmemt of congruence may be more problematic between the preferred collective goals or solutions and the proposed strategies and tactics of the various groups involved. There could be sharp differences within leadership groups regarding the most suitable goals for the movement, as for instance between more radical or moderate solutions, these differences being at times dependent on the leaders' assessments of the views, often more moderate, of potential and actual followers. The same goes with regard to the most effective tactics and strategies to be adopted to reach these goals. Framing construction in this regard could often turn out to be much more complex and energy consuming, and could easily lead to internal confrontations.

Much effort is also likely to be demanded from leaders and militants to align their likely expectations of success, one of Gamson's framing components. The expectations of success of followers will often be weaker than those of leaders and activists, and the latter, through rituals and speeches, will have to constantly work to revive or strengthen the optimism of the first, given that no collective action is possible without a necessary sense of political efficacy.

Notice, however, that within the framing tasks discussed by Snow et al. (1986), no attention is paid to some of the other components of the model of motivation presented. Framings, especially, of simple aspirations, whether acceptable or not, and of selective incentives also have to be attended to by leaders and other militants; feelings of moral obligations are only briefly discussed within the frame amplification process.

Some of the four strategic alignment processes are likely to play more important roles with regard to the dynamics of motivation. While the assessments of grievances and relevant emotions may be relatively congruent in many instances, feelings about them could very well be much amplified by framing efforts. The amplification could even be more pronounced with regard to the emotions derived from grievances, although they may have at times to be transformed, as mentioned above. Our presumptions would be that bridging, and even the other framing processes, would play a less important role with regard to these components. Conversely, frame transformation could take place more often regarding the persons to whom the blame should be attributed.

The sense of moral obligation is probably the motivational component most often subjected to framing amplification efforts on the part of movement leaders and militants. Depending on the amount of sacrifices anticipated and the stages of participation, there could be much variability in their likely presence and in their salience: the sacrifices implied could easily be relatively less onerous in the early stages of participation and a sense of duty easily accepted, but gradually the demands could become very substantial, so that felt obligation could develop into the main internal push to action, a form of amplification of beliefs discussed by Snow et al. (1986, 471–2). Finally, movement efforts may often have to be directed to the frame transformation of simple aspirations into the gradual development of a sense of moral obligation.

As implied above, much frame transformation or extension of the collective incentives pursued may have at times to be negotiated, since "an smo may have to encompass interests or points of view that are incidental to its primary objectives, but of considerable salience to potential adherents" (Snow et al. 1986, 472). As for selective incentives, movement leaders will often have to amplify the importance of low-cost social gratifications, given their limited resources for the provision of material ones.

Finally, with regard to expectancy of success, it is imperative, as argued by those writers, for movements to counter pessimistic expectations, given their temporal variability and their necessity, by the frame amplification of realistic possibilities of success. In addition, given the circumstances, this framing work could bear on short-term partial gains or on ultimate goal attainment, depending on which of these appears most salient to members.

The framing claims of challengers will be constantly questioned in their opponents' counter framings; the latter could question the seriousness of the articulated grievances and could especially argue that the collective goods pursued, if realized, would be accompanied by greater collective bads and that at any rate their chances of success would be minimal, if not non-existent. The effectiveness of such efforts could be great among uncommitted bystanders, but they could also undermine the motivations of still hesitant adherents. Hence the importance given by both sides to such framing tasks.

While there have been a good number of studies concerned with the validation of the presumed effects of framing on various movement processes and outcomes (for a review of these studies, see Snow 2004; Benford and Snow 2000), there is only a very limited amount of evidence on the impact of framing on motivation proper, and it comes mainly from the initiators of that perspective.

Gamson (1992a) has presented detailed results in his study bearing on the presence of each element of his collective action frame – injustice, agency, and identity – in peer group conversations of working people on four major issues – affirmative action, nuclear power, troubled industry, and the Arab-Israeli conflict. It is fascinating to observe how fragments of each element of the frame emerged spontaneuosly in conversations on some of the issues. This was not of course very frequent, and when present, the emerging elements were not necessarily well integrated or shared by many; often they presented ambiguities. With regard to agency, a lot of cynicism was expressed regarding the possibilty of change. All in all, the injustice frame emerged more easily and turned out to be a critical catalyst for the appearance of the other two elements. But given that the conversations were occurring outside of any meaningful collective action context – something deemed crucial for the development of a frame – one should not be surprised that "full-fledged collective action frames that integrated all three elements were rare indeed" (111).

The impact of frame alignment processes on many more components of motivation was empirically examined by Snow et al. (1986), largely on the basis of data these authors had collected on religious, peace, and neighborhood movements (see also Benford and Snow 2000 for other instances). In line with what was suggested earlier, the greatest impact was exercised through the amplification process: amplification of the grievances (threats) to family and neighborhood values and to women and children expressed against homeless, transient males in the neighborhood movements and to democratic values in the peace movement; amplification of notions of moral obligation and duty in the peace movement and in the Nichiren Shoshu movement; amplification of beliefs in efficacy and expectancies of success in the neighborhood and peace movements again. The process of frame extension was also found to be at work, to include the material grievances of minority groups with the usual concerns of the peace movement activists or to add the potential social selective incentives of prospective recruits to the more central concerns of militants in the religious movements. Finally, frame transformation from narrow to much wider collective incentives were reported in relation to the peace and Nichiren Shoshu movements. In short, these results suggest that the effects of framing on the emergence and development of social movements can be often facilitated through modifications of some of the motivational dimensions involved.

THE ROLE OF COLLECTIVE IDENTITIES

In general, the emergence of contentious collective action is likely to be accompanied by the salience of existing collective identities or the creation of new ones, reinforcing the action. The concept of collective identity, like that of solidarity, widely used in studies of contentious action, are very closely related to one another and in fact are often used interchangeably (see Hunt and Benford 2004 for a discussion of these concepts). The concept of solidarity has for long retained the attention of sociologists, but during recent decades, the concept of collective identity received greater attention, possibly because it can be held to be a source of solidarity (Gamson, Fireman, and Rytina 1982, 22; Polletta and Jasper 2001, 291). *Collective identity* refers to sentiments among members of a group that they share much with one another regarding their values, goals, interests, and fate, thus giving rise to "we" feelings. These sentiments in turn produce feelings of *solidarity*, as sentiments of great interdependence between the members of the group in the pursuit of these shared components.

Collective identities increasingly came to be seen as crucial determinants of the emergence and growth of collective protest, as alternatives to structurally given political and economic interests or to selective incentives as determinants (Polletta and Jasper 2001). Indeed Snow and McAdam (2000, 41) went so far as to assert that "identity is the key concept in social movement research today" (also Melucci 1989, chap. 1).

Collective identities could be rooted in many embedded layers. Gamson (1992a) identified three relevant layers: the organization sponsoring the action (e.g., the Congress of Racial Equality), the larger social movement of which the organization is a part (the Civil Rights movement), or the even larger community of people that the social movement is claiming to represent (the American Black community) (see also Jasper 1997, 85–90, for an alternaitve set of layers). Collective identities could remain weak for long periods and even subsist without much consciousness of their presence; it is only when they become very salient that they exert strong effects.

Collective identities do not only constitute cognitive assessments. Their definition as shared *sentiments* clearly implies that they involve emotions, frequently deep ones in fact, as argued by authors stressing the importance of emotions in analyses of social movements. Jasper (1998, 415) wrote that "most of all, [collective identity] is an emotion," and that "the 'strength' of an identity comes from its emotional side" (see also Jasper 1997; Goodwin, Jasper, and Polletta 2001, 8–10; Gould 2002, 191–2; Van Stekelenburg and Klandermans 2007, 164). But such emotions not only follow the emergence of collective identities; Taylor and Rupp (2002) showed that before the Second World War a pre-existing *emotion culture* was antecedent to the construction of an international feminist collective identity by transnational women's organizations.

The prime concern of this section is with the impact of collective identities – implying also solidarity – on the various dimensions of motivation distinguished in the model of motivation, although the reverse relationships, with those dimensions affecting collective identities, will also be considered. Most of the literature, however, is concerned with both the impact of collective identities on contentious action in general, not on motivation specifically, and on the reversed impact of action on identities; these propositions cannot therefore be overlooked and they will be briefly examined presently.

Let me first state that the assumption regarding these two-way relationships is presumably valid. Although often implicitly recognized, they have rarely been explicitly discussed; but Gamson (1992a, 6–7 and endnote 1), Jasper (1997, 192), and Polletta and Jasper (2001, 290–2) did express that possibility. Collective identities could precede as well as emerge gradually as a result of collective action. The emergence and growth of social movements and participation in them, especially those based on communal groups defined by race or ethnicity, class, religion, gender, or the like, are likely to be greatly facilitated by pre-existing collective identities, while in issue movements, like ecology, peace, disarmement, pro-life, or pro-abortion, identities follow, as a result of their action.[1] When they are pre-existing, salient collective identities tend to lead to very rapid mobilization. Needless to say, whether pre-existing or not, identities are not stable: in the dynamics of collective action, through framing and collective action itself, as well as through the strategic efforts of leaders, they are subjected to constant processes of amplification, consolidation, expansion, and transformation (Snow and McAdam 2000; Benford and Snow 2000).

Many discussions of collective identities deal with their impact on collective action, not on the reversed impact of the action on identities. This should not be too surprising, since interest in that dimension stemmed mostly from their presumed strong effects on participation.[2] Earlier studies (Gamson 1975; Fireman and Gamson 1979) were more limited, dealing with the impact of solidarity on action, with solidarity claimed to be an alternative to Olson's selective incentives, an issue critically examined in chapter 4.

Studies discussing the impact of identities and solidarity on action are numerous, and most of them present empirical evidence. Among the early and strongest claims bearing specifically on identity, one finds Gamson's (1992a) inclusion of collective identity in his collective action frame. Klandermans (1997, chap. 2) in turn adopted the components of Gamson's frame as core motivational dimensions in his analysis of the determinants of adherence to a movement. Subsequently, in somewhat modified models, collective identities still remained a central mechanism, with the straightforward hypothesis "overwhelmingly supported" that strong group identification made action participation more likely (Klandermans 2004, 364–5; Van Stekelenburg and Klandermans 2007; Klandermans, Van der Toorn, Van Stekelenburg 2008).

The reversed impact of mobilization on identity is a central tenet of the new social movements approach. Melucci (1980, 1981, 1988, 1989) remains the most influential representative of that perspective. For him not only are collective identities a result stemming from the pursuit of some materialistic goods, but above all their construction becomes the goal of the action itself (see chap. 1; see also Gamson 1992b; Snow and Oliver 1995). Although this is accepted by Melucci (1989), American students of social movements, especially of the women's movements, more clearly recognized the importance of both materialistic and symbolic goals and assumed identity construction to be a constantly evolving and changing process of two-way relationships. Verta Taylor and her collaborators are excellent representatives of such views. They could show that identities in lesbian feminist collectivities, rooted in gender domination, might precede the action but then be further strengthened in subsequent mobilization (Taylor and Whittier 1992). Conversely international women's organizations could generate new international feminist identities, this being greatly facilitated by previous emotion labour, and these developments facilitating in turn their action for women's rights and peace (Taylor and Rupp 2002). Similar processes are described in two episodes of mobilization regarding same-sex weddings (Taylor, Kimport, Van Dyke, and Andersen 2009). This is also elaborated in Staggenborg and Taylor's (2005) and Staggenborg and Lecomte's (2009) excellent studies, where social movement communities, more or less in abeyance, are distinguished from active social movement campaigns and where the construction of identities and motivation in the communities set the stage for mobilization in subsequent campaigns, in turn enhancing identities. Finally, Klandermans (1997, 51–2) made the important point that collective action enhances the identities not only of movement participants but also those of sympathetic bystanders, not to mention the conflicting identities of their opponents.

The studies of those authors are not the only ones. There are many others, generally also focussing, at least implicitly, on two-way relationships (Gurr 1993a,b; Snow and Oliver 1995; Snow and McAdam 2000; Hunt and Benford 2004; Kurtz 2002; Jasper 1997; Polletta and Jasper 2001; Goodwin and Jasper 2004; Gould 2002; Kawakani and Dion 1993; Simon et al. 1998; Stürmer, Simon, Loewy, and Jörger 2003). Notice in particular that identification with a movement organization was found by Simon et al.(1998) to exert a stronger effect on participation than identification with the overall collectivity that the organization claims to represent.

The literature offers, however, very few discussions of the impact of dual or multiple identities, whether parallel or divergent. Parallel multiple identities refer to those shared by different subgroups within a challenging group (or within the opponent group), as for instance women in the civil rights movement. Kurtz (2002) has shown that parallel identities – in her study, multiple identities as workers, women, and blacks within a challenging labour union – created difficulties, since their organization could not easily integrate and respond to all identities at once. As expected from a union, a labour conflict pitted mostly its members as aggrieved workers against their employers, with less attention to grievances specific to women and blacks, despite the fact that these two groups were in the majority in the union. In such cases, these latter identities tend to lose much of their salience, with reduced impact on mobilization.

Divergent multiple – usually dual – identities occur when some members of a collectivity develop identities with both potential challengers and opponents. As an instance of dual divergent identities, one can cite the case of the Quebec Francophones who maintain identities both with their linguistic group and with the whole Canadian collectivity, while others identify only with one of these groups, either Francophones or Canadians. When mobilization for the pursuit of Quebec independence developed around 1960, those with single identities with one or the other group could of course more easily join in the respective collective action of each, but those with divided loyalties were much more likely to remain on the sidelines or to become only weak participants in one of the camps. The patterns of identities showed constant modifications during the following decades. Actually, one important part of the mobilization efforts on each side was to try to change people's identities in their favour (Pinard 1980, 1997a, 1997b; Nadeau and Fleury 1995; on other cases of dual identities, see Klandermans, Van der Toorn, and Van Stekelenburg, 2008, 995). The literature, however, remains too overly concentrated on the construction of challengers' single identities and their evolution.

Turning to our main concern, the impact of collective identities on various motivational dimensions, the issue has not received as much attention. This is all the more surprising since *motivations can be assumed to be a most important mechanism linking identities to collective action.* The idea that motivation could act as such a mechanism is generally disregarded in the literature, except for Van Stekelenburg and Klandermans (2007, 181–2) and Stürmer, Simon, Loewy, and Jörger's (2003, 78–9) discussion of some indirect or mediating effects of motivational factors.

Probably the most important impact of collective identities on motivation concerns the generation or strengthening of a sense of moral obligation – and of the emotion of pride in conforming to it – increasing one's motives to participate; this was first argued in the solidarity section of chapter 4. Few others have discussed that. Jasper (1997, 136) did argue that "every form of identity ... carries certain moral obligations," and Stürmer et al. (2003) empirically verified that an inner obligation to behave as a good member of the group mediated between identity and social movement participation (see also Polletta and Jasper 2001, 290; Van Stekelenburg and Klandermans 2007, 184).

Collective identities can also exert intensifying effects on another central internal motive, that is, grievances and their accompanying emotions, particularly when these are just emerging and barely developed. Like emotions (Van Stekelenburg and Klandermans 2007, 183), identities could very well be said to act as amplifiers, if not accelerators, of the impact of grievances on action. Taylor and Whittier (1992, 105) are among the few authors mentioning the identity-grievances relationship, writing that "identity construction processes are crucial to grievance interpretation in all forms of collective action." And Kurtz (2002, 67) argued that collective identity helps to translate conditions of injustice into such action. Similar claims are found in Gurr (1993a) and in Kawakani and Dion (1993), the latter providing empirical evidence linking salient collective identity to group relative deprivation.

Finally, such identities could greatly dampen the role of our third internal motive, *simple aspirations*. The greater the salience of identities, the more difficult it would be for opportunistic actors to pursue self-interested goals; under salient identities such actions would be viewed even more negatively and become subject to severe selective disincentives.

Identities also bear relationships to some external incentives. Friedman and McAdam (1992) even argued that during the emergence phase of a movement, activist identities could themselves contitute cheap, but powerful, selective incentives for participants, while at later phases such identities could provide only collective incentives, inciting to free-ride. Regarding other selective incentives, collective identities and their affective dimensions could make participation a source of pleasure (Jasper 1998, 415), and these identities could themselves generate emotional satisfaction (Polletta and Jasper 2000, 290). With regard to selective disincentives, identities could increase the costs of defection (Klandermans 2004, 368). In addition they could enhance the value of potential collective gains (Jasper 1998, 415).

Finally, expectancy of success could also be intensified by identities (Jasper 1997, 88). Kelly (1993) reported that strong group identification facilitated collective action by promoting shared perceptions of the possibility of social change. Collective identities could even transform emotions of resignation into feelings of anger and the like.

There are obvious reasons why a reversed effect of grievances on identities could be expected. Shared experiences of grievances by members of a collectivity could easily lead its members to develop sentiments of shared fate in important dimensions of their life, that is, feelings of collective identity. The close association between grievances and collective identity "lies in the fact that the organization of how social movements adherents think about themselves is structured in important ways by how shared wrongs are experienced, interpreted, and reworked in the context of group interaction" (Johnston, Larana, and Gusfield 1994, 22). Put differently, the assessment in diagnostic framing of what is wrong facilitates "the construction of both protagonist and antagonist identity fields" (Hunt, Benford, and Snow 1994; also Hunt and Benford 2004). There are empirical results supporting such views. In a study of the gay movement in the United States, it was found that when the common fate of gays as a threatened minority was made salient, it increased identification with the gay movement (Simon et al. 1998). Similarly, gender inequality and domination were described as a source of lesbian identity construction (Taylor and Whittier 1992). The claim that serious grievances and accompanying emotions could engender salient collective identities has also been made by Gurr (1993a, 126), with analogous claims made by Klandermans (1997, 41).

In short, the essential point is that salient collective identities do not only exert strong effects on collective action – and vice versa – in some direct way, but also indirectly, by first intensifying the scope of most components of motivation, with these constituting key mechanisms for the impact of identities on various processes of collective action. This is therefore an additional reason to consider problems of motivation seriously.

CONCLUSIONS

The arguments of this book have moved us far beyond the simple traditional arguments according to which either deprivations or collective interests are the essential motivating forces in contentious collective action. Not only must a valid perspective consider both of them, but in addition it must take into account that they come in variable combinations with other components, unfortunately more complex combinations than one would have liked.

With regard to grievances, our detailed review of the empirical evidence and of the methodological flaws often encountered in some studies has, I hope, undermined the pervasive doubts about their central relevance. Moreover more subtle considerations of the role of aspirations and of moral obligation should enlarge any future debate regarding motivational perspectives in contentious politics. As external pulling forces, collective and selective incentives must be clearly differentiated, the first being all too often confused with the second, specifically when they refer to the particular collective goods pursued by subgroups within a larger constituency. Finally expectancy of success is a component that ought to occupy a central place in any motivational model. One cannot overstate that when it is absent, a very large number of potential challengers remain paralyzed.

Much empirical research has yet to be carried out to verify the validity of the model presented. Only the beginning of such efforts, reviewed in previous chapters, has been made, especially in Pinard and Hamilton (1986).

But needless to say, motivational factors are far from being the only determinants of contentious collective action. Many other determinants of a social-psychological nature, particularly when affecting motivation, ought to be the object of serious considerations, such as problems related to processes of framing and of collective identification. Above all, motivational perspectives remain to be incorporated within more general structural frameworks.

Notes

1 For more detailed distinctions between different types of deprivations or grievances, see chap. 4.

2 For a classic study of a movement done within that tradition, one that emphasizes deprivations, specifically status threats, see Gusfield's study of the American temperance movement (Gusfield 1963).

3 Given, as will be seen, the importance of "meanings" attached to objective strains in subsequent theories, it ought to be mentioned that this notion was already present in Smelser's generalized beliefs (16), despite their shortcomings.

4 It is therefore incorrect to hold, as is often done, that explanations of the emergence of movements in all early perspectives "pointed to sudden increases in individual grievances generated by the 'structural strains' of rapid social change" (Jenkins 1983, 528).

5 Collective incentives were not completely ignored in Smelser, since objectives and goals of the action were considered within the generalized belief component. Indeed the same could be said about the analyses of goals in previous approaches.

6 For a rather negative view of even Smelser's analytical model, see Rule (1988).

7 In addition to the criticisms of the relative deprivation theory for its overemphasis on deprivation, there have been also criticisms of the empirical work based on that perspective, such as improper measurements of the concept – its reliance on aggregate data only – and the

presumed lack of supportive evidence. As will be shown later, when properly measured, relative deprivation proved a very relevant factor.

8 Grievances and demands were, however, usually indiscriminately lumped together. See also Gurr (1993b) for an interesting quantitative test of that model, with data on more than 200 minority ethnic groups from all over the world. Unfortunately the measure of mobilization remains a rather simple one, and no measures of opportunities are provided.

9 For an interesting study showing that some of the immediate determinants of a sense of grievances (feelings of dissatisfaction with one's life conditions) are to be found in objective deprivations (race and class), as well as in subjective conditions (relative deprivations and sense of justice), and how these interact and change, see Klandermans, Roefs, and Olivier (2001). On this question, see also Gurr (1993b, 178–9).

10 Despite the criticisms to follow, the important contributions of those approaches regarding mobilization problems are fully recognized, such as, among others, the structural bases of recruitment, the importance of resource flows for action, the contributions of outside groups and institutions, the role of political opportunities and coercion, the formation and break-up of coalitions, the determinants and impact of strategies and tactics, and the dynamic political processes of movement growth and decline.

11 Let me reassert, however, that social integration can exert both restraining and mobilizing effects, not only the latter, a position too often neglected (Pinard 1975). Let me also mention that while deprivation belongs to the motivation cluster, disintegration and integration belong to the organization one.

12 For similar criticisms, see in particular Gamson (1987).

13 In his discussion of framing later on in the same book, Zald (1996, 268–9) did, however, make a few remarks concerning the role of grievances.

14 Even within motivation, they lumped together under the demands for change such disparate elements as "sentiments, preferences, tastes, values, grievances" (ibid., 536). Note how grievances come last.

15 In their discussion of lethal conflicts, for instance, they discard any serious role for motives as a "motivation fallacy" (137). It is interesting to note that the book starts with two brief narratives of episodes of contentious politics. A first episode is the campaign against the slave

trade in eighteenth-century England, and a second one, the Orange Revolution in Ukraine in 2004. Now, it is striking that the first epi-sode involved old, relatively constant deprivations, which therefore could not have spurred the campaign. The second episode, however, is said to have started in reaction to an electoral fraud (as in Serbia and Georgia earlier), that is, to sudden new grievances, piling up over older ones. This major difference, which contradicts their frequent claims, is entirely missed in the subsequent analysis.

16 As discussed in chapter 4, the competition theory of ethnic conflict is another approach starting simply with interests, the presence of which is assumed, and moving to other factors (for a good example, see Niel-sen 1985).

17 As mentioned below, something approaching such concerns does appear in one of Tilly's major books (1978), but only in his discussion of revolutions.

18 As, for instance, in the "collective *interest* model" of Finkel and Muller (1998), which indeed treats internal discontents more fully than exter-nal collective goods.

19 Indeed, as noted by Piven and Cloward (1992, 307–8), concessions to deprivation arguments are always more frequent in Tilly's empir-ical work (as well as in the work of others from the same persuasion). Thus in his work on collective violence in Europe (Tilly, Tilly, and Tilly 1975, 271–2), a distinction is made in the conclusion between short-term hardships and durable grievances, with the position, contrary to Marx, that it is the latter that are important, although Snyder and Tilly (1972, 520) had earlier conceded that short-term hardships could precipitate rebellion. Similarly, in his work with Shorter on strikes in France (Shorter and Tilly 1974), there are repeated concessions to short-term hardship and deprivation arguments only for them to be negated in subsequent paragraphs – despite their rather positive evi-dence to be reviewed below. Indeed they had explicitly rejected both absolute and relative deprivation from the start (8).

20 Before that revision, McAdam, in his new introduction to *Political Process and the Development of Black Insurgency* (1999) had already argued that in Tilly's early component of opportunity/threat, threat had become increasingly neglected in favour of opportunity and that threat ought to be restored as an equally important factor. See also Van Dyke and Soule (2002).

21 Notice that Tilly (1978, 134–5) had already hypothesized, quite rightly, that responses to threats were likely to be stronger than responses to opportunities, the first implicitly assumed to create grievances, the second, to simply generate aspirations. It should also be noted that given that threats are often new, anticipated harms, they are more likely than actual deprivations, which are often stable, to represent changing situations and therefore triggering factors of collective action.

22 For the revised position of this last author, see, for instance, his recent joint paper on African-American protest (Jenkins, Jacobs, and Agnone 2003).

23 See also Tarrow (1989b), who discusses the role of grievances in the ascending phase of movement cycles.

24 A second mechanism of regime defection that is mentioned is "infringement of elite interests." Is this not often also a form of suddenly imposed grievances?

25 As Koopmans (2003) counted them, at least forty-four mechanisms were proposed in this book. But with only one involving grievances, it shows the limited attention given to them. Moreover, in the condensed sequel to this book (Tilly and Tarrow 2007), this mechanism was no longer mentioned.

26 Thus while adding framing processes to their agenda, McAdam, Tarrow, and Tilly (2001, 16) write that "social actors frame their claims, their opponents and their identities." But what about framing their grievances, which is seen as the first and crucial task of framing (see below)?

27 Similarly, although Hechter (2000, 8) rejects the importance of motives as inscrutable, resistant to accurate survey measures, and not good predictors of behavior anyway, he subsequently makes recurrent references to (assumed) grievances, threats, and discontents in his explanations of nationalism.

28 For instance, the first edition of Turner and Killian's *Collective Behavior* (1957) contained thirteen chapters on elementary forms of collective behavior, but only eight on social movements.

29 This was the case with many communal movements (e.g., the US civil rights movement, the Quebec independence movement, and other ethnoregional movements, and the women's, student, and gay liberation movements), as well as with some single-issue movements (e.g.,

the ecology, the pro-choice movements), although other single-issue movements were often responses to new grievances (e.g., anti-war, peace, and anti-nuclear movements). But there were also during that period movements of working-class protest also triggered by increasing grievances (e.g., the populist Social Credit Party in Quebec).

30 It has to be mentioned that authors often working outside the traditional confines of the social movements literature have usually considered deprivation arguments as highly relevant in their structural models. An important, classic instance of this is the central place given to the economic deprivations of a boom and bust economy in Lipset's work on agrarian protest in Saskatchewan (Lipset 1950). More generally, in his comparative analysis of left voting among the lower classes, Lipset (1960, chap. 7) considered deprivations as central in a general scheme including both deprivations and structural facilitating conditions. Such a multidimensional approach, if taken seriously by current structural theorists, would have led them to avoid the pitfalls just discussed (Von Eschen 1989). Another, more recent example of deprivation is Goldstone's model of state breakdown and revolution (1991, chap. 6), in which a major trend, population growth, leads, among other things, to grievances among displaced elite groups and to mass deprivations of various kinds.

31 Notice how Melucci (1980, 217) rejected the breakdown vs solidarity alternative as a false problem, breakdown being seen as leading to deprivations and to collective action born out of solidarity.

32 As will be seen, collective identities alone would not constitute motives to engage in collective action in the absence of any other motivational dimensions.

33 However, Benford and Snow (2000, 615–16), while recognizing that injustice frames were commonplace in many types of social movements, disagreed with Gamson's assertions (1992b; 1992a) that all "collective action frames are injustice frames" or that at least they all contain an injustice component. They claimed it was questionable to make such an assertion in the case of many religious, self-help, and identity movements, even though that appeared ubiquitous in movements for political and/or economic change. This implies the need to enlarge the notion of grievance to include, for instance, the types of discontents so central in the new social movements approach, as done by Klandermans (1997, 40) and in the definitions presented above.

34 Notice that the prognostic framing of solutions here corresponds to the formulation of collective incentives in structural approaches.

35 Benford, an early proponent of the framing perspective, subsequently joined his voice to those of the critics (Benford 1997).

36 Jasper (1998, 398) actually refers to emotions as "appropriate feelings," and Gould (2004, 161) writes about "grievances ... deeply felt" to refer to emotions discussed in early theories. See also Benford (1997, 419) for similar remarks.

37 It would have been more accurate, following Ferree and Merrill (2004, 252), to oppose cold cognitions to hot emotions.

38 Fear, stressed by Lofland, as just mentioned, is an important emotion, particularly in situations of threats, and should be listed with anger and indignation, central in Gamson (Aminzade and McAdam 2001, 31).

39 For instance the concepts of deprivation and grievance are rarely mentioned in Jasper (1987) and are totally absent in Jasper (1998). Notice, however, that the concept of threat, defined here as anticipated deprivation, is used profusely with reference to the emotions accompanying them.

40 Is it because in their view, rather questionable, the concepts of grievance used by many imply mainly cognitive connotations? Or because threats immediately refer to external situations, particularly in many of the examples they give, while grievances refer to internal feelings, a notion reserved for emotions?

41 See also my earlier criticisms, although based on different grounds, of Tilly's recourse to the concept of threat.

42 While at one point Jasper distinguished (so-called) threats based on already developed problems and prospective threats based on uncertain futures (1997, 128), that distinction is generally ignored. Thus he listed layoffs, plant closings, and wage cuts, which are clearly already developed deprivations, as examples of economic threats (1997, 117). Incidentally, at times threats are confusingly said to be one of three emotions, together with fear and outrage (1997, 129; also Goodwin, Jasper, and Polletta 2000, 77).

43 The reference here is of course to primarily reactive emotions, as mentioned before. Affective emotions can of course increase a sense of threat and its reactive emotions.

44 There are even mentions that a sense of threats could follow, as when it is asserted that "a sense of threat must be built out of raw emotions like fear, dread, and hate" (Jasper 1997, 116).

45 Emotions should also of course be integrated with other cultural and structural factors, such as acquired values and ideologies, collective identifications, framing processes, social embeddedness, opportunities, and strategic mobilization efforts; this will be examined later.

46 Both Van Zomeren et al. (2004) and Klandermans et al. (2008) report that the effects of anger appeared to be much stronger than the effects of observed unfairness; the latter is, however, a measure not of felt grievances but only of observed deprivations, which can be assumed to exert weaker effects to start with.

CHAPTER TWO

1 For excellent analyses of the early processes through which injustice frames and full collective action frames develop among unorganized potential challengers, see Gamson, Fireman, and Rytina (1982) and Gamson (1992a).

2 For detailed studies of such a case, see Pinard and Hamilton 1986 and Mendelsohn, Parkin, and Pinard 2007.

3 Note that in a recent longitudinal study of African-American protest, Jenkins, Jacobs, and Agnone (2003) observed that the grievances they measured were not constant, and they found them to be significant factors in the occurrence of protest.

4 It is rather ironic that while levels of organization are frequently stable, even more so than levels of deprivations, political process theorists never argue that organization is irrelevant.

5 Or even more so, if they are declining, in particular during periods of affluence. The obvious point here is that those deprivations may not have completely disappeared, that the decline may not be well perceived, or that other deprivations remain. For a discussion of this problem in the case of the Quebec independence movement, see Pinard and Hamilton (1986), where it is shown that there has been a substantial decrease in the economic disadvantages of francophones, but few changes in the perception of those disadvantages, and as seen, no changes overall in felt deprivations of various kinds (e.g., ones of status).

6 Notice that in some of the studies cited, the deprivations involved were displaced rather than relevant (e.g., economic deprivations of Whites participating in the Black movement), although the former were obviously only secondary determinants. But even family tensions and conflicts have been found to be related to children's participation in a student craze (Cooper 1968) or in the student movement (Wood 1974, chap. 7; see also Parkin 1968).

7 For those more easily convinced by qualitative studies, see also the very vivid descriptive study of a right-wing political movement that, during the great depression, took only a few years to come to power in Alberta (Irving 1959). For a few other qualitative studies of ethnoregional movements, see Pinard 2002, 249–50.

8 But see Sokol's supportive data with a measure of *felt* status inconsistency, cited by Lipset (1963, 403).

9 Moreover, while the latter relationship practically disappeared with trust in political authorities controlled, this does not imply spuriousness: relative deprivation caused distrust, which in turn led to support for contentious collective action.

10 In the second study, the effect of racial dissatisfaction on willingness to use violence was even stronger (a difference of 44 percent), although it combined the effects of racial dissatisfaction and powerlessness. (The original study (Ransford 1968) had already reported a strong zero-order effect of racial dissatisfaction.) In the third study, only partially reported, positive, but weak, relationships were observed. It is astonishing that Muller (1972, 929n) referred to Crawford and Naditch's findings with the latter's own data as showing only "moderate" to "weak" relationships, and that later McCarthy and Zald (1977, 1214) went one step further, citing both Muller's as well as Crawford and Naditch's papers as showing "little or no support" for the expected deprivation relationships.

11 The only unexpected finding is the last one, but the current level of relative deprivation of these respondents is not known. Again, Muller (1972, 930n) presented this study as showing only a weak association between relative deprivation and protest orientation (a statement that is correct only when social mobility is not controlled), and McCarthy and Zald listed it with the others as showing little or no support for the deprivation hypothesis. (Indeed McCarthy and Zald are accurate only with regard to the fourth study they cited, that of Snyder and Tilly 1972).

12 For instance, in Gamson's (1975, 112) study, it was reported that close to three-fourths (74 percent) of the American challenging groups that emerged between 1810 and 1945 did so during "periods of social unrest," excluding wars, which covered less than half the period studied. Reanalyzing those data, Goldstone (1980a, 1040) found a weaker, non-significant relationship between occurrence and crisis periods, but the latter included wars, during which, according to Gamson (1975) and Tilly, Tilly, and Tilly (1975), contentious collective action was less likely to occur. See also the supportive study of Davies (1962), although it is of a more qualitative kind.

13 A study of the aggregate results of surveys of US urban riots from 1956 to 1968 also provided negative evidence concerning Davies' J-curve hypothesis, but the authors suggested an alternative deprivation hypothesis in terms of ambiguity and uncertainty (with regard to the respondents' financial situation) (Miller, Bolce, and Halligan 1977).

14 The presentation will be limited to findings concerning strike frequency (rather than strike duration or size), since this appears to be the most relevant dimension here (Walsh 1975, 46–8). For an excellent study of all these dimensions that responded differently to various factors, see Franzosi 1995.

15 Notice that Jenkins, Jacobs, and Agnone (2003, 284) failed to take into account the distinction between the negative effect of unemployment on strikes, because it reduced workers' opportunities, and its positive effect on many other types of protest, where its deprivation effect was unimpaired by such negative opportunities.

16 The latter found that in France striking significantly increased with lower real wages and greater industrial production in five of the seven regression or path analysis results presented for various periods – despite some problems to be discussed presently. This indeed forced Shorter and Tilly (1974, 102–3) to revise their model in order to introduce a so-called "short-term hardship" determinant, since deprivation had been altogether left out of their original model (77). But with Snyder, they keep insisting that organizational (unionization) and political factors were then much more important than economic factors, though the evidence is not unambiguous, particularly with regard to political factors.

17 Notice that while in Markoff's study, economic deprivations were not factors of rural revolt in 1789 France, political grievances produced by market incorporation and bureaucratic intrusion had strong effects.

18 Indeed in that study, to the expressed surprise of the author, the solidarity hypothesis, not the grievance one, failed to be supported by the data. Could this have been owing to the lack of variation in solidarity?

19 These two categories of participants are analogous to the categories of voters with rebellious and retreatist alienation (Pinard 1975, 241).

20 Collier and Hoeffler label one of their measures as political exclusion or dominance, but it measures only the majority status of the larger ethnic group.

21 Wimmer and his colleagues found political exclusion effects in all civil wars, not only in ethnic ones, and in particular in ethnic rebellions. Notice that they also found that the number of ethnic groups involved in sharing power arrangements – something that does not necessarily imply ethnic grievances – to be the source of another form of violent conflict, namely elite infighting, this one much less frequent, but rooted in competition. More about this in chapter 4.

CHAPTER THREE

1 Another example. In a recent study of immigrants' protest participation, Klandermans, Van der Toorn, and Van Stekelenburg (2008) lumped together actions with a general goal and actions with goals specific to immigrants, something which may have affected some of their results, since the two types of action may respond to different factors.

2 See Gouldner's (1954) for an impressive case study of a defensive wildcat strike and of the important role played by non-economic grievances, but not by the workers' organization. For subsequent recognitions of the necessity to disaggregate the dependent variables, see Snyder (1979), Christman, Kelly, and Galle (1981, 83), and Sambanis (2001).

3 It is interesting to note that when they start disaggregating their data and using more appropriate measures of deprivation, the Tillys uncover some positive findings, as in the relation between high (presumably food) prices and food riots in France during the pre-1860 period (1975, 75).

4 Some of these criticisms have often been made (e.g., Davies 1974; Smith 1979). Indeed Gurr and Duvall (1973, 136–8) recognized that the indicators used were often partial, indirect, and even dubious, and

acknowledged that they had not previously been measuring relative deprivation. To Davies' critique (1974) of a lack of match between the deprivation data and the groups acting, Snyder and Tilly (1974), in their rejoinder, acknowledged that the admonition was "substantial" (611) but went on to say that the same problems also generally plagued the relative deprivation research. That is correct, but two faulty procedures do not make for a right one.

5 It also of course disappears in the presentations of early approaches drawn by their critics.

6 In this discussion, I assumed that deprivation was the necessary motivating factor. We shall see below that other internal motives could replace deprivations; moreover, even when deprivation is involved, positive external incentives and expectancy of success must also be present. This implies that it should be more difficult to observe strong zero-order relationships between deprivation and participation.

7 In this regard, consider Isaac, Mutran, and Stryker's (1980) findings that both absolute and relative deprivation were significantly related to protest orientations among Blacks, but not among Whites. Apart from measurement problems, which may possibly account for this difference, it is interesting to note that in that study, only Blacks were exposed to constant active mobilization: the city (Gary, Indiana, in 1969) had been the site of important Black protest during the 1960s and had recently been one of the first large U S cities to elect a Black mayor. Hence with mobilization present only for Blacks, deprivation was found to have had an impact only among them.

8 In Jenkins' study, mobilization efforts are properly assumed (implicitly) to have been present throughout Russia during the short number of very turbulent years considered (1905–7). Hence peasant communities with higher levels of relevant grievances were more likely to engage in revolt than others. Conversely, in Lieberson and Silverman's study of riots over a period of fifty-one years, riot communities that had been mobilized were paired with non-riot communities that (presumably) had not been, since mobilization was unlikely to have been constant over such a long time. The authors found that on most measures of economic deprivation, there were no differences between riot and non-riot cities. Given the necessity of mobilization and its presumed absence from many deprived communities, the absence of riots in the latter does not appear surprising.

9 For an interesting effort to also measure the impact of conduciveness, see Snyder (1979).

10 Note that it is only in such a multivariate analysis that a significant hardship relationship appears (Snyder and Tilly 1972, 529).

11 There is one type of longitudinal studies that escape this pitfall by simply being, interestingly enough, imperfect longitudinal ones. These studies indicate, in line with the deprivation hypothesis, that "challenging groups" (Gamson 1975) have tended in the past to emerge during hard times. As the analysis here starts not from all time units but from the actual occurrences of such groups, the researchers are in situations akin to those of participation studies researchers: mobilization has taken place and hence a deprivation/emergence relationship can be observed.

12 Lipset's (1950) study of the rise of the CCF in Saskatchewan is an excellent example of an analysis showing the impact of a high and stable level of organization for the rise of a political movement under the increasing hardships of the great depression.

13 Many of the points just raised would be relevant to account for the inconsistent findings found in the literature on strikes, but such an analysis is beyond the scope of this chapter.

CHAPTER FOUR

1 Or, as Gamson (1975, 56) puts it, the distinguishing characteristic of collective goods is "that one receives the 'benefits,' dubious or real, whether one has paid for them and wants them or not."

2 As will be seen, aspirations can of course easily be transformed into grievances when one feels that one's aspirations are being unjustly blocked.

3 Von Eschen (1989) presents a detailed review of studies with at least implicit aspiration arguments. His review and further discussions with him were important in my writing of this section.

4 In the case of Collier and Hoeffler, see other studies of civil wars challenging their claims in chapter 2. On the shortcomings of the competition model, see Bélanger and Pinard (1991).

5 Notice that while political exclusion was directly measured in the case of ethnic rebellions, competition in the case of infightings was only inferred from the presence of multiple ethnic groups participating in

existing power arrangements. Whether that competition was predominantly rooted in aspirations or in the grievances of some of the competitors, something not unrealistic in such radical competition, is ignored.

6 Routine and contentious collective action should be seen not as clearly distinct modes of action but as the two poles of a continuum.

7 There are no doubt exceptions, such as small groups of rebels engaging in coups d'état on the sole basis of their power aspirations pursued because of favorable opportunities.

8 Net collective goods must be considered, since both goods and bads could be incurred as a result of the action.

9 See my discussion of Wimmer, Cederman, and Min's (2009) position on this issue in chapter 1.

10 There is also Gamson's (1975, chap. 5) finding that challenging groups offering selective incentives were more likely to be successful than others, although implications of motivation in this case would be more remote and although reanalyses of the same data by Steedley and Foley (1979) and by Goldstone (1980a) failed to support that finding; indeed Goldstone found that selective incentives retarded the success of challenging groups.

11 For an important emphasis placed on ideology in a social-psychological perspective, see Ferree and Miller (1985). Zald (1996) subsequently paid serious attention to the role of ideology.

12 Ideal deprivations are distinct from material ones; they refer to gaps between existing conditions and sets of ideals, while material ones refer to deprivations of material goods of an economic, status, or power nature.

13 But adherence to moral values is not irrelevant, since this kind of moral testimony can in particular convince others and ultimately increase participation (Jasper 1997, 136–7)

14 As pointed out by these authors, "hard" selective incentives of a material or social kind involve positive and negative sanctions that are mediated by the group and affect the situation of the actor, while the "soft" ones are internalized incitations, working simply on the orientation of the actor. It could be added that the former are often problematic, while the latter necessarily follow from one's compliance with moral obligations.

15 If altruism was not involved, one would observe fewer participants desisting from participation with the argument that "they had done

their share." From their literature review, Piliavin and Charng's (1990) claimed that a paradigm shift has occurred away from assertions that altruism is ultimately self-interested. But for a different notion of altruism, in which it is considered as part of self-interest rather than contrasted to self-interest, see Marwell (1982).

16 Consistent with this, Klandermans (1984, 597) suggested that instead of my imputed role of moral obligations, an alternative solution to Olson's dilemma could be provided by expectancy of success, specifically by expectations that others will participate. But Klandermans (1997, 81) also claimed that this would be relevant only under an accelerating production function, something that already solves the free-riding problem, so that the expectations about others would only increase the probability of participation.

17 Klandermans (1997, 81) wrote that both collective and selective incentives were necessary in that form of collective action. My conclusions therefore differ, with the first being necessary and sufficient when only moral obligations are involved, and the second, when only self-interest prevails.

18 It will be seen below, however, that they are highly relevant in many indirect ways.

19 Some elementary forms of participation, such as voting or signing a petition, involve costs that are so small that they are more akin to adherence than to participation (Pinard and Hamilton 1986; Klandermans 1997, 64).

20 This should not be confused with the hypothesis that the support-deprivation relationship should be stronger under mobilization than in its absence, as discussed in the previous chapter.

21 This would be the case even if all were to have the same perceptions about their grievances, which is not the case.

22 This interdependence is also considered in Atkinson's theory of achievement motivation (Atkinson and Feather 1966, 359–60; Feather 1982b).

23 Expectancy of success and political efficacy have slightly different meanings. The first refers to perceptions of the group's *chances* of success, the second to perceptions of the group's *capacity* to succeed. It can be argued that the sense of political efficacy is an important determinant of expectancy of success, with the latter being the crucial motivating factor in collective action.

CHAPTER FIVE

1 The motivation model to be presented is primarily concerned with social movements and other forms of contentious collective action. But there are no discontinuities between the latter and more routine forms of collective action, and the model could just as well apply to the latter, although of course the mix of motivational components would be quite different.

2 In Korpi's model, Atkinson's theory is employed to specify the mechanisms through which controlled power resources are mobilized for action. The only components of motivation retained are relative deprivations as internal motives, the actor's expected collective costs of reaching the goal, as external incentives – the latter two determining the utility of reaching that goal – and expectancy of success.

3 In subsequent multiplicative models, Muller and his colleagues considered general grievances and expectancy of success as components (Finkel and Muller 1998; Muller, Dietz, and Finkel 1999), with the addition of selective incentives in the first study and of moral obligation in the second.

4 Thus, to take Blalock's example, "if there is no need (e.g., hunger is satisfied), *or* no expectation of success, *or* no external reward (food), then no behavior directed toward this objective will take place" (1967, 34; italics in original).

5 Some of these distinctions are borrowed from Von Eschen (1989). Ideal deprivations stem from contradictions between one's ideals and current conditions, while material ones simply reflect one's material conditions; relevant deprivations are those the collective action aims to resolve, while displaced ones are outside the action purview, but bring one toward the action anyway; soft deprivations refer to all kinds of personality disorders, while all other deprivations are considered as hard.

6 As, for instance, when the shortage or high prices of food led to participation in protests bearing on altogether different issues (Rudé 1964, 219).

7 The deprivations are shared ones experienced by most members of a group. The consciousness of this sharing need not be widespread from the start, since this is something to be developed through framing. By contrast, it is not believed that the sum of many idiosyncratic

deprivations (e.g., the marriage problems of A, the boring job of B, the psychological hang-ups of C, and the like) could in any way be important motives of participation, although some of them could be secondary motivating elements for some participants.

8 Note that moral obligations are internal motives, while principles are generally presented as external incentives replacing selective ones.

9 The emotions tied to grievances are the ones most often considered in the literature.

10 To the extent that at least some degree of decelerating and of accelerating production functions prevail at the same time in a given form of action, then all three equations would combine additively.

11 Oberschall's (1980) model shows more difference. While considering the role of collective and selective incentives and expectancy of success, it formally neglects the role of all internal motives.

12 They add social embeddedness as a fifth element, but it is of a social, not a motivational, nature.

13 Thus, for instance, Hechter (2000, 71) claims that in multicultural societies, peripheral elites' challenges are based on grievances regarding their loss of power and privileges, while peripheral masses respond to a cultural division of labour. (This of course neglects the other motivational components.)

14 Conscience constituents are supporters who do not stand to benefit directly from a movement's accomplishments, contrary to its beneficiary base.

15 The greater attention paid to leaders by proponents of structural approaches may therefore contribute to the greater role they attribute to the pursuit of collective goods.

16 Compare this with Oliver (1989, 14–16), who suggested that in populations with long enduring grievances at very high levels, such grievances will be weak predictors of participation when compared to populations without enduring high grievance levels. The issue is what one considers as very high and enduring grievance levels that are debilitating and those that are not. Among Quebec Francophones, to give but one example, the levels of felt grievances are enduring and high, but they are still strongly related to participation (Pinard and Hamilton 1986).

CHAPTER SIX

1 These latter types of action could, however, gain from "movement" identities (Jasper 1997, 192).

2 Goodwin and Jasper (2000, 24) even write that identities are logically prior to the action, since participants must know who they are before getting involved. This is less certain in the case of issue movements.

References

Aiken, Michael, Louis A. Ferman, and Harold L. Sheppard. 1968. *Economic Failure, Alienation, and Extremism.* Ann Arbor: University of Michigan Press.

Amenta, Edwin, and Yvonne Zylan. 1991. "It Happened Here: Political Opportunity, the New Institutionalism, and the Townsend Movement." *American Sociological Review* 56:250–65.

Aminzade, Ron, and Doug McAdam. 2001. "Emotions and Contentious Politics." In *Silence and Voice in the Study of Contentious Politics*, edited by R.R. Aminzade et al., 14–50. New York: Cambridge University Press.

Ashenfelter, Orley, and George E. Johnson. 1969. "Bargaining Theory, Trade Unions, and Industrial Strike Activity." *American Economic Review* 59:35–49.

Atkinson, John W. 1964. *An Introduction to Motivation.* Princeton: Van Nostrand.

Atkinson, John W., and Norman T. Feather. 1966. "Review and Appraisal." In *A Theory of Achievement Motivation*, edited by J.W. Atkinson and N.T.Feather, 327–70. New York: Wiley.

Beck, E.M., and Stewart E. Tolnay. 1990. "The Killing Fields of the Deep South: The Market for Cotton and the Lynching of Blacks, 1882–1930." *American Sociological Review* 55:526–39.

Bélanger, Sarah, and Maurice Pinard. 1991. "Ethnic Movements and the Competition Model: Some Missing Links." *American Sociological Review* 56:446–57.

Benford, Robert D. 1997. "An Insider's Critique of the Social Movement Framing Perspective." *Sociological Inquiry* 67:409–30.

Benford, Robert D., and David A. Snow. 2000. "Framing Processes and Social Movements: An Overview and Assessment." *Annual Review of Sociology* 26:611–39.

Biggs, Michael. 2006. "Who Joined the Sit-ins and Why: Southern Black Students in the Early 1960s." *Mobilization* 11:241–56.

Blais, André, Pierre Martin, and Richard Nadeau. 1995. "Attentes économiques et linguistiques et appui à la souveraineté du Québec." *Canadian Journal of Political Science* 28:637–57.

Blalock, Hubert M., Jr. 1967. *Toward a Theory of Minority-Group Relations*. New York: Wiley.

Bloombaum, Milton. 1968. "The Conditions Underlying Race Riots as Portrayed by Multidimensional Scalogram Analysis: A Reanalysis of Lieberson and Silverman's Data." *American Sociological Review* 33:76–91.

Blumer, Herbert. 1955. "Collective Behavior." In *Principles of Sociology*, edited by A.M. Lee, 165–222. New York: Barnes and Noble.

Boldt, Menno. 1981. "Philosophy, Politics, and Extralegal Action: Native Indian Leaders in Canada." *Ethnic and Racial Studies* 4:205–21.

Bowen, Don R., Elinor Bowen, Sheldon Gawiser, and Louis H. Masotti. 1968. "Deprivation, Mobility, and Orientation toward Protest of the Urban Poor." In *Riots and Rebellion: Civil Violence in the Urban Community*, edited by L.H. Masotti and D.R. Bowen, 187–200. Beverly Hills, CA: Sage.

Breton, Albert, and Raymond Breton. 1969. "An Economic Theory of Social Movements." *The American Economic Review* 59:198–205.

– 1980. *Why Disunity? An Analysis of Linguistic and Regional Cleavages in Canada*. Montreal: The Institute for Research on Public Policy.

Breton, Raymond. 1972. "The Socio-Political Dynamics of the October Events." *Canadian Review of Sociology and Anthropology* 9:33–56.

– 1998. "Ethnicity and Race in Social Organization: Recent Developments in Canadian Society." In *The Vertical Mosaic Revisited*, edited by R. Helmes-Hayes and J. Curtis, 60–115. Toronto: University of Toronto Press.

Breton, Raymond, and Daiva Stasiulis. 1980. "Linguistic Boundaries and the Cohesion of Canada." In *Cultural Boundaries and the Cohesion of Canada*, edited by R. Breton, J.G. Reitz, and V. Valentine, 137–323. Montreal: The Institute for Research on Public Policy.

Buhaug, Halvard, Lars-Erik Cederman, and Jan Ketil Rod. 2008. "Disaggregating Ethno-Nationalist Civil Wars: A Dyadic Test of Exclusion Theory." *International Organization* 62:531–51.

Caplan, Nathan. 1970. "The New Ghetto Man: A Review of Recent Empirical Studies." *Journal of Social Issues* 26:59–73.

Carden, Maren Lockwood. 1978. "The Proliferation of a Social Movement: Ideology and Individual Incentives in the Contemporary Feminist Movement." *Research in Social Movements, Conflicts, and Change* 1:179–96.

Cedernan, Lars-Erik, and Luc Girardin. 2007. "Beyond Fractionalization: Mapping Ethnicity onto Nationalist Insurgencies." *American Political Science Review* 101:173–85.

Centers, Richard. 1961 [1949]. *The Psychology of Social Classes: A Study of Class Consciousness*. New York: Russell and Russell.

Christman, Lillian J., William R. Kelly, and Omer R. Galle. 1981. "Comparative Perspectives on Industrial Conflict." *Research in Social Movements, Conflicts and Change* 4:67–93. Greenwich, CT: JAI Press.

Collier, Paul, and Anke Hoeffler. 2004. "Greed and Grievance in Civil War." *Oxford Economic Papers* 56:563–95.

Cooper, Robert M. 1968. *Beatlemania: An Adolescent Countraculture.* MA thesis, McGill University.

Cousineau, Jean-Michel, and Robert Lacroix. 1976. "Activité économique, inflation et activité de grève." *Industrial Relations Industrielles* 31:341–58.

Crawford, Thomas J., and Murray Naditch. 1970. "Relative Deprivation, Powerlessness, and Militancy: The Psychology of Social Protest." *Psychiatry* 33:208–23.

Crossley, Nick. 2002. *Making Sense of Social Movements*. Philadelphia: Open University Press.

Cuneo, Carl J., and James E. Curtis. 1974. "Quebec Separatism: An Analysis of Determinants within Social Class Levels." *Canadian Review of Sociology and Anthropology* 11:1–29.

Currie, Elliott, and Jerome H. Skolnick. 1970. "A Critical Note on Conceptions of Collective Behavior." *The Annals of the American Academy of Political and Social Science* 391:34–45.

Davies, James C. 1962. "Toward a Theory of Revolution." *American Sociological Review* 27:5–19.

– 1974. "The J-Curve and Power Struggle Theories of Collective Violence." *American Sociological Review* 39:607–10.

Downes, Bryan T. 1968. "Social and Political Characteristics of Riot Cities: A Comparative Study." *Social Science Quarterly* 49:504–20.

– 1970. "A Critical Reexamination of the Social and Political Characteristics of Riot Cities." *Social Science Quaterly* 51:349–60.

Fearon, James D., Kimuli Kasara, and David D. Laitin. 2007. "Ethnic Minority Rule and Civil War Onset." *American Political Science Review* 101:187–93.

Fearon, James D., and David D. Laitin. 2003. "Ethnicity, Insurgency, and Civil War." *American Political Science Review* 97:75–90.

Feather, Norman T. 1982a. "Actions in Relation to Expected Consequences." In *Expectations and Actions: Expectancy-Value Models in Psychology,* edited by N.T. Feather, 53–95. Hillsdale, NJ: Lawrence Erlbaum.

– 1982b. "Expectancy-Value Approaches: Present Status and Future Directions." In *Expectations and Actions: Expectancy-Value Models in Psychology,* edited by N.T. Feather, 395–420. Hillsdale, NJ: Lawrence Erlbaum.

– 1990. "Bridging the Gap between Values and Actions." In *Handbook of Motivation and Cognition: Foundations of Social Behavior*, vol. 2, edited by E.T. Higgins and R.M. Sorrentino, 151–92. New York: Guilford Press.

Feierabend, Ivo K., and Rosalind L. Feierabend. 1972. "Systemic Conditions of Political Aggression: An Application of Frustration-Aggression Theory." In *Anger, Violence and Politics: Theories and Research*, edited by I.K. Feierabend, R. L. Feierabend, and T. R. Gurr, 136–83. Englewood Cliffs, NJ: Prentice-Hall.

Feierabend, Ivo K., Rosalind L. Feierabend, and Betty A. Nesvold. 1969. "Social Change and Political Violence: Cross-National Patterns." In *Violence in America: Historical and Comparative Perspectives*, edited by H.P. Graham and T.R. Gurr, 606–67. New York: The New American Library.

Ferree, Myra Marx, and David A. Merrill. 2004. "Hot Movements, Cold Cognition: Thinking about Social Movements in Gendered Frames." In *Rethinking Social Movements: Structure, Meaning, and Emotion,* edited by J. Goodwin and J.M. Jasper, 247–61. Lanham, MD: Rowman and Littlefield.

Ferree, Myra Marx, and Frederick D. Miller. 1985. "Mobilization and Meaning: Toward an Integration of Social Psychological and Resource Perspectives on Social Movements." *Sociological Inquiry* 55:38–51.

Finkel, Steven E., and Edward N. Muller. 1998. "Rational Choice and the Dynamics of Collective Political Action: Evaluating Alternative Models with Panel Data." *American Political Science Review* 92:37–49.

Fireman, Bruce, and William A. Gamson. 1979. "Utilitarian Logic in the Resource Mobilization Perspective." In *The Dynamics of Social Movements: Resource Mobilization, Social Control, and Tactics,* edited by M.N. Zald and J.D. McCarthy, 8–44. Cambridge, MA: Winthrop Publishers.

Flacks, Richard. 1967. "The Liberated Generation: An Exploration of the Roots of Student Protest." *Journal of Social Issues* 23:52–75.

Ford, William Freithaler, and John H. Moore. 1970. "Additional Evidence on the Social Characteristics of Riot Cities." *Social Science Quarterly* 51:339–48.

Frank, Joseph A., and Michael Kelly. 1977. "Etude préliminaire sur la violence collective en Ontario et au Québec, 1963–1973." *Canadian Journal of Political Science* 10:145–57.

– 1979. "Street Politics in Canada: An Examination of Mediating Factors." *American Journal of Political Science* 23:593–614.

Franzosi, Roberto. 1995. *The Puzzle of Strikes: Class and State Strategies in Postwar Italy.* New York: Cambridge University Press.

Freeman, Jo. 1973. "The Origins of the Women's Liberation Movement." *American Journal of Sociology* 78:792–811.

Friedman, Debra, and Doug McAdam. 1992. "Collective Identity and Activism: Networks, Choices, and the Life of a Social Movement." In *Frontiers in Social Movement Theory,* edited by A.D. Morris and C.M. Mueller, 156–73. New Haven: Yale University Press.

Gamson, William A. 1975. *The Strategy of Social Protest.* Homewood, IL: The Dorsey Press.

- 1980. "Understanding the Careers of Challenging Groups: A Commentary on Goldstone." *American Journal of Sociology* 85:1043–60.
- 1987. "Introduction." In *Social Movements in an Organizational Society: Collected Essays*, edited by M.N. Zald and J.D. McCarthy, 1–7. New Brunswick: Transaction Books.
- 1992a. *Talking Politics*. New York: Cambridge University Press.
- 1992b. "The Social Psychology of Collective Action." In *Frontiers in Social Movement Theory*, edited by A.D. Morris and C.M. Mueller, 53–76. New Haven: Yale University Press.

Gamson, William A., Bruce Fireman, and Steven Rytina. 1982. *Encounters with Unjust Authority*. Homewood: The Dorsey Press.

Goldstone, Jack A. 1980a. "The Weakness of Organization: A New Look at Gamson's *The Strategy of Social Protest*." *American Journal of Sociology* 85:1017–42.
- 1980b. "Mobilization and Organization: Reply to Foley and Steedly and to Gamson." *American Journal of Sociology* 85:1428–32.
- 1991. *Revolution and Rebellion in the Early Modern World*. Berkeley: University of California Press.

Goldstone, Jack A., and Charles Tilly. 2001. "Threat (and Opportunity): Popular Action and State Response in the Dynamics of Contentious Action." In *Silence and Voice in the Study of Contentious Politics*, edited by R.R. Aminzade et al., 179–94. New York: Cambridge University Press.

Goodwin, Jeff, and James M. Jasper. 2004. "Caught in a Winding, Snarling Vine: The Structural Bias of Political Process Theory." In *Rethinking Social Movements: Structure, Meaning, and Emotion*, edited by J. Goodwin and J.M. Jasper, 3–30. Lanham, MD: Rowman and Littlefield.

Goodwin, Jeff, James M. Jasper, and Francesca Polletta. 2000. "The Return of the Repressed: The Fall and Rise of Emotions in Social Movement Theory." *Mobilization* 5: 65–84.
- 2001. "Why Emotions Matter." In *Passionate Politics: Emotions and Social Movements*, edited by J. Goodwin, J.M. Jasper, and F. Polletta, 1–24. Chicago: University of Chicago Press.
- 2004. "Emotional Dimensions of Social Movements." In *The Blackwell Companion to Social Movements*, edited by D.A. Snow, S.A. Soule, and H. Kriesi, 1–24. Malden, MA: Blackwell Publishing.

Gould, Deborah B. 2002. "Life during Wartime: Emotions and the Development of ACT UP." *Mobilization* 7:177–200.

– 2004. "Passionate Political Processes: Bringing Emotions Back into the Study of Social Movements." In *Rethinking Social Movements: Structure, Meaning, and Emotion,* edited by J. Goodwin and J.M. Jasper, 155–75. Lanham, MD: Rowman and Littlefield.

Gouldner, Alvin W. 1954. *Wildcat Strike.* Yellow Springs, OH: The Antioch Press.

Grofman, Bernard N., and Edward N. Muller. 1973. "The Strange Case of Relative Gratification and Potential for Political Violence: The v-Curve Hypothesis." *American Political Science Review* 67:514–39.

Guimond, Serge, and Lise Dubé-Simard. 1983. "Relative Deprivation Theory and the Quebec Nationalist Movement: The Cognition-Emotion Distinction and the Personal-Group Deprivation Issue." *Journal of Personality and Social Psychology* 44:526–35.

Gurr, Ted Robert. 1968. "A Causal Model of Civil Strife: A Comparative Analysis Using New Indices." *American Political Science Review* 62:1104–24.

– 1970. *Why Men Rebel.* Princeton: Princeton University Press.

– 1993a. *Minorities at Risk.* Washington: United States Institute of Peace Press.

– 1993b. "Why Minorities Rebel: A Global Analysis of Communal Mobilization and Conflict since 1945." *International Political Science Review* 14:161–201.

Gurr, Ted Robert, and Raymond Duvall. 1973. "Civil Conflict in the 1960s: A Reciprocal Theoretical System with Parameter Estimates." *Comparative Political Studies* 6:135–69.

Gusfield, Joseph R. 1963. *Symbolic Crusade: Status Politics and the American Temperance Movement.* Urbana: University of Illinois Press.

Hall, O. Milton. 1934. "Attitudes and Unemployment: A Comparison of the Opinions and Attitudes of Employed and Unemployed Men." *Archives of Psychology* 25:1–65.

Hamilton, Richard F. 1967. *Affluence and the French Worker in the Fourth Republic.* Princeton: Princeton University Press.

Hardin, Russell. 1993. "Altruism and Mutual Advantage." *Social Service Review* 67:358–73.

– 1995. *One for All: The Logic of Group Conflict*. Princeton: Princeton University Press.

Hechter, Michael. 2000. *Containing Nationalism*. New York: Oxford University Press.

Heirich, Max. 1977. "Change of Heart: A Test of Some Widely Held Theories about Religious Conversion." *American Journal of Sociology* 83:653–80.

Hibbs, Douglas A., Jr. 1973. *Mass Political Violence: A Cross-National Causal Analysis*. New York: Wiley.

– 1976. "Industrial Conflict in Advanced Industrial Societies." *American Political Science Review* 70:1033–58.

Hirsch, Eric L. 1990. "Sacrifice for the Cause: Group Processes, Recruitment, and Commitment in a Student Social Movement." *American Sociological Review* 55:243–54.

Horowitz, Donald. 1985. *Ethnic Groups in Conflict*. Berkeley: University of California Press.

Hovland, Carl I., and Robert R. Sears. 1940. "Minor Studies of Aggression: VI. Correlation of Lynchings with Economic Indices." *Journal of Psychology* 9:301–10.

Hunt, Scott. A., and Robert D. Benford. 2004. "Collective Identity, Solidarity, and Commitment." In *The Blackwell Companion to Social Movements*, edited by D.A. Snow, S.A. Soule, and H. Kriesi, 432–57. Malden, MA: Blackwell Publishing.

Hunt, Scott. A., Robert D. Benford, and David A. Snow. 2004. "Identity Fields: Framing Processes and the Social Construction of Movement Identities." In *New Social Movements: From Ideology to Identity,* edited by E. Larana, H. Johnston, and J. R. Gusfield, 185–208. Philadelphia: Temple University Press.

Inglehart, Ronald. 1990. *Culture Shift in Advanced Industrial Society*. Princeton: Princeton University Press.

– 1995. "Public Support for Environmental Protection: Objective Problems and Subjective Values in 43 Societies." *PS: Political Science & Politics* 28:57–72.

Irvine, William P. 1972. "Recruitment to Nationalism: New Politics or Normal Politics?" *Canadian Journal of Political Science* 5:503–20.

Irving, John A. 1959. *The Social Credit Movement in Alberta*. Toronto: University of Toronto Press.

Isaac, Larry, Elizabeth Mutran, and Sheldon Stryker. 1980. "Political Protest Orientations among Black and White Adults." *American Sociological Review* 45:191–213.

Jasper, James M. 1997. *The Art of Moral Protest: Culture, Biography, and Creativity in Social Movements*. Chicago: The University of Chicago Press.

– 1998. "The Emotions of Protest: Affective and Reactive Emotions in and around Social Movements." *Sociological Forum* 13:397–424.

– 2006. "Motivation and Emotion." In *The Oxford Handbook of Contextual Political Analysis,* edited by R.E. Goodin and C. Tilly, 157–71. New York: Oxford University Press.

Jenkins, J. Craig. 1981. "Sociopolitical Movements." In *The Handbook of Political Behaviour,* vol. 4, edited by S.L. Long, 81–153. New York: Plenum.

– 1982. "Why Do Peasants Rebel? Structural and Historical Theories of Modern Peasant Rebellions." *American Journal of Sociology* 88:487–514.

– 1983. "Resource Mobilization Theory and the Study of Social Movements." *Annual Review of Sociology* 9:527–53.

Jenkins, J. Craig, David Jacobs, and Jon Agnone. 2003. "Political Opportunities and African-American Protest, 1848–1997." *American Journal of Sociology* 109:277–303.

Jenkins, J. Craig, and Charles Perrow. 1977. "Insurgency of the Powerless: Farm Worker Movements, 1946–1972." *American Sociological Review* 42:249–68.

Jiobu, Robert M. 1971. "City Characteristics, Differential Stratification and the Occurrence of Interracial Violence." *Social Science Quarterly* 52:508–20.

– 1974. "City Characteristics and Racial Violence." *Social Science Quarterly* 55:52–64.

Johnston, Hank, Enrique Larana, and Joseph R. Gusfield. 1994. "Identities, Grievances, and New Social Movements." In *New Social Movements: From Ideology to Identity,* edited by E. Larana, H. Johnston, and J.R. Gusfield, 3–35. Philadelphia: Temple University Press.

Jurkat, Ernest H., and Dorothy B. Jurkat. 1949. "Economic Function of Strikes." *Industrial and Labor Relations Review* 2:527–45.

Kawakami, Kerry, and Kenneth L. Dion. 1993. "The Impact of Salient Self-Identification on Relative Deprivation and Action Intentions." *European Journal of Social Psychology* 23:525–40.

Kelly, Caroline. 1993. "Group Identification, Intergroup Perceptions, and Collective Action." *European Review of Social Psychology* 4:59–83.

Kennan, John. 1986. "The Economics of Strikes." In *Handbook of Labor Economics*. Vol 2, edited by O. Ashenfelter and R. Layard, 1091–1137. New York: Elsevier.

Kerbo, Harold R. 1982. "Movements of 'Crisis' and Movements of 'Affluence.'" *Journal of Conflict Resolution* 26:645–63.

Klandermans, Bert. 1984. "Mobilization and Participation: Social-Psychological Expansions of Resource Mobilization Theory." *American Sociological Review* 49:583–600.

– 1988. "The Formation and Mobilization of Consensus." In *From Structure to Action: Comparing Social Movement Research across Cultures,* edited by B. Klandermans, H. Kriesi, and S. Tarrow, 173–96. Greenwich, CT: JAI Press.

– 1997. *The Social Psychology of Protest*. Cambridge, MA: Blackwell Publishers.

– 2004. "The Demand and Supply of Participation: Social-Psychological Correlates of Participation in Social Movements." In *The Blackwell Companion to Social Movements*, edited by D.A. Snow, S.A. Soule, and H. Kriesi, 360–79. Malden, MA: Blackwell Publishing.

Klandermans, Bert, and Dirk Oegema. 1987. "Potentials, Networks, Motivations, and Barriers." *American Sociological Review* 52:519–31.

Klandermans, Bert, Marlene Roefs, and Johan Olivier. 2001. "Grievance Formation in a Country in Transition: South Africa, 1994–1998." *Social Psychology Quarterly* 64:41–54.

Klandermans, Bert, and Sidney Tarrow. 1988. "Mobilization into Social Movements: Synthesizing European and American Approaches." In *From Structure to Action: Comparing Social Movement Research Across Cultures,* edited by B. Klandermans, H. Kriesi, and S. Tarrow, 1–38. Greenwich, CT: JAI Press.

Klandermans, Bert, Jojanneke van der Toorn, and Jacquelien van Stekelenburg. 2008. "Embeddedness and Identity : How Immigrants

Turn Grievances into Action." *American Sociological Review* 73:992–1012.

Koopmans, Ruud. 1996. "Explaining the Rise of Racist and Extreme Right Violence in Western Europe : Grievances or Opportunities." *European Journal of Political Research* 30:185–216.

– 2003. "A Failed Revolution – but a Worthy Cause." *Mobilization* 8:116–19.

Kornhauser, William. 1959. *The Politics of Mass Society*. New York: Free Press.

Korpi, Walter. 1974. "Conflict, Power and Relative Deprivation." *American Political Science Review* 68:1569–78.

Kousis, Maria, and Charles Tilly. 2005. "Economic and Political Contention in Comparative Perspective." In *Economic and Political Contention in Comparative Perspective*, edited by M. Kousis and C. Tilly, 1–11. Boulder: Paradigm Publishers.

Kowalchuk, Lisa, and Maurice Pinard. 1993. "The New Middle Class, the Intellectuals and Quebec's Independence Movement: An Empirical Assessment." Paper presented at the Annual Meeting of the Canadian Sociology and Anthropology Association, Ottawa.

Kurtz, Sharon. 2002. *Workplace Justice: Organizing Multi-Identity Movements*. Minneapolis: University of Minnesota Press.

Ladner, Robert A., Barry J. Swartz, Sandra Roker, and Loretta S. Titterud. 1981. "The Miami Riots of 1980: Antecedent Conditions, Community Responses and Participant Characteristics." *Research in Social Movements, Conflicts and Change* 4:171–214.

LeBon, Gustave. 1960 [1895]. *The Crowd: A Study of the Popular Mind*. New York: Viking.

LeCavalier, Patricia F. 1983. "Resourceful Movements: The Mobilization of Citizens for Neighbourhood Planning Control." PH D diss., McGill University.

Leggett, John C. 1964. "Economic Insecurity and Working-Class Consciousness." *American Sociological Review* 29:226–34.

Lenski, Gerhard E. 1966. *Power and Privilege: A Theory of Social Stratification*. New York: McGraw-Hill.

Lieberson, Stanley, and Arnold R. Silverman. 1965. "The Precipitants and Underlying Conditions of Race Riots." *American Sociological Review* 30:887–98.

Lieske, Joel A. 1978. "The Conditions of Racial Violence in American
    Cities: A Developmental Synthesis." *American Political Science
    Review* 72:1324–40.

Lipset, Seymour Martin. 1950. *Agrarian Socialism: The Cooperative
    Commonwealth Federation in Saskatchewan.* Berkeley: University of
    California Press.

– 1960. *Political Man.* Garden City, New York: Doubleday.

– 1963. "Three Decades of the Radical Right: Coughlinites,
    McCarthyites, and Birchers." In *The Radical Right,* edited by D.
    Bell, 373–446. Garden City, NY: Doubleday Anchor.

– 1971. *Rebellion in the University.* Boston: Little, Brown.

Lofland, John. 1985. *Protest: Studies of Collective Behavior and Social
    Movements.* New Brunswick, NJ: Transaction Books.

Lord, Guy, Daniel Latouche, and Denis Lacorne. 1976. "Les organisa-
    teurs électoraux et autre travailleurs d'élections." In *Le processus
    électoral au Québec: Les élections provinciales de 1970 et 1973,*
    edited by D. Latouche, G. Lord, and J.-G. Vaillancourt, 77–91.
    Montréal : Hurtibuse HMH.

Low-Beer, John R. 1978. *Protest and Participation: The New Working
    Class in Italy.* Cambridge: Cambridge University Press.

Markoff, John. 1985. "The Social Geography of Rural Revolt at the
    Beginning of the French Revolution." *American Sociological Review*
    50:761–81.

Marwell, Gerald. 1982. "Altruism and the Problem of Collective
    Action." In *Cooperation and Helping Behavior: Theories and
    Research,* edited by V.J. Derlega and J. Grzelak, 207–26. New York:
    Academic Press.

Marwell, Gerald, and Pamela Oliver. 1993. *The Critical Mass in
    Collective Action: A Micro-Social Theory.* New York: Cambridge
    University Press.

Marx, Gary T. 1967. *Protest and Prejudice: A Study of Belief in the
    Black Community.* New York: Harper and Row.

– 1970. "Issueless Riots." *The Annals of the American Academy of
    Political and Social Science* 391:21–33.

Marx, Gary T., and James L. Wood. 1975. "Strands of Theory and
    Research in Collective Behavior." *Annual Review of Sociology*
    1:363–428.

Matthews, Donald R., and James W. Prothro. 1966. *Negroes and the New Southern Politics*. New York: Harcourt, Brace.

McAdam, Doug. 1988. *Freedom Summer*. New York: Oxford University Press.

– 1999 [1982]. *Political Process and the Development of Black Insurgency 1930–1970*. 1st and 2d eds. Chicago: University of Chicago Press.

– 2001. "Harmonizing the Voices: Thematic Continuity across the Chapters." In *Silence and Voice in the Study of Contentious Politics*, edited by R.R. Aminzade et al., 222–40. New York: Cambridge University Press.

– 2003. "Beyond Structural Analysis: Towards a More Dynamic Understanding of Social Movements." In *Social Movements and Networks*, edited by M. Diani and D. McAdam, 281–98. New York: Oxford University Press.

McAdam, Doug, John D. McCarthy, and Mayer N. Zald. 1988. "Social Movements." In *Handbook of Sociology*, edited by N. Smelser, 695–737. Newbury Park: Sage Publications.

– 1996. "Introduction: Opportunities, Mobilizing Structures, and Framing Processes – towards a Synthetic, Comparative Perspective on Social Movements." In *Comparative Perspectives on Social Movements: Political Opportunities, Mobilizing Structures, and Cultural Framings*, edited by D. McAdam, J.D. McCarthy, and M.N. Zald, 1–20. New York: Cambridge University Press.

McAdam, Doug, and David A. Snow. 1997. "Conditions of Strain: Conflict and Breakdown." In *Social Movements*, edited by D. McAdam and D.A. Snow, 2–4. Los Angeles: Roxbury.

McAdam, Doug, Sidney Tarrow, and Charles Tilly. 2001. *Dynamics of Contention*. New York: Cambridge University Press.

McCarthy, John D., Mark Wolfson, David P. Baker, and Elaine Mosakowski. 1988. "The Founding of Social Movement Organizations: Local Citizens' Groups Opposing Drunken Driving." In *Ecological Models of Organizations*, edited by G.R. Carroll, 71–84. Cambridge, MA: Ballinger Publishing Company.

McCarthy, John D., and Mayer N. Zald. 1973. *The Trend of Social Movements in America: Professionalization and Resource Mobilization*. Morristown, NJ: General Learning Press.

– 1977. "Resource Mobilization and Social Movements: A Partial Theory." *American Journal of Sociology* 82:1212–41.

– 2002. "The Enduring Vitality of the Resource Mobilization Theory of Social Movements." In *Handbook of Sociological Theory*, edited by J.H. Turner, 533–65. New York: Kluwer Academic/Plenum Publishers.

McEvoy, III, James. 1971. *Radicals or Conservatives? The Contemporary American Right*. Chicago: Rand McNally.

McPhail, Clark. 1971. "Civil Disorder Participation: A Critical Examination of Recent Research." *American Sociological Review* 36:1058–73.

Melson, Robert, and Howard Wolpe. 1970. "Modernization and the Politics of Communalism: A Theoretical Perspective." *American Political Science Review* 64:1112–30.

Melucci, Alberto. 1980. "The New Social Movements: A Theoretical Approach." *Social Science Information* 19:199–226.

– 1981. "Ten Hypotheses for the Analysis of New Movements." In *Contemporary Italian Sociology: A Reader*, edited by D. Pinto, 173–94. Cambridge: Cambridge University Press.

– 1988. "Getting Involved: Identity and Mobilization in Social Movements." In *From Structure to Action: Comparing Social Movement Research across Cultures*, edited by B. Klandermans, H. Kriesi, and S. Tarrow, 329–48. Greenwich, CT: JAI Press.

– 1989. *Nomads of the Present: Social Movements and Individual Needs in Contemporary Society*. Philadelphia: Temple University Press.

Mendelsohn, Matthew. 2003. "Rational Choice and Socio-Psychological Explanation for Opinion on Quebec Sovereignty." *Canadian Journal of Political Science* 36:511–37.

Mendelsohn, Matthew, Andrew Parkin, and Maurice Pinard. 2007. "A New Chapter or the Same Old Story?" In *Quebec and Canada in the New Century*, edited by M. Murphy, 25–52. Montreal: McGill-Queen's University Press.

Millar, David, and Maurice Pinard. 1998. "Sustained Participation and Disengagement in the Parti Québécois." Paper presented at the Annual Meetings of the Canadian Sociology and Anthropology Association, Ottawa.

Miller, Abraham H., Louis H. Bolce, and Mark Halligan. 1977. "The J-Curve Theory and the Black Urban Riots: An Empirical Test of Progressive Relative Deprivation Theory." *American Political Science Review* 71:964–82.

Mintz, Alexander. 1946. "A Re-Examination of Correlations between Lynchings and Economic Indices." *Journal of Abnormal and Social Psychology* 41:154–60.

Morgan, William R., and Terry Nichols Clark. 1973. "The Causes of Racial Disorders: A Grievance Level Explanation." *American Sociological Review* 38:611–24.

Morrison, Denton E., and Allan D. Steeves. 1967. "Deprivation, Discontent, and Social Movement Participation: Evidence on a Contemporary Farmers' Movement, the NFO." *Rural Sociology* 32:414–34.

Mueller, Carol McClurg. 1992. "Building Social Movement Theory." In *Frontiers in Social Movement Theory,* edited by A.D. Morris and C.M. Mueller, 3–25. New Haven: Yale University Press.

Muller, Edward N. 1972. "A Test of a Partial Theory of Potential for Political Violence." *American Political Science Review* 66:928–59.

– 1979. *Aggressive Political Participation.* Princeton: Princeton University Press.

Muller, Edward N., Henry A. Dietz, and Steven A. Finkel. 1991. "Discontent and the Expected Utility of Rebellion: The Case of Peru." *American Political Science Review* 85:1261–82.

Muller, Edward N., and Thomas O. Jukam. 1983. "Discontent and Aggressive Political Participation." *British Journal of Political Science* 13: 159–79.

Muller, Edward N., and Mitchell A. Seligson. 1987. "Inequality and Insurgency." *American Political Science Review* 81:425–51.

Myers, Daniel J. 1997. "Racial Rioting in the 1960s: An Event History Analysis of Local Conditions." *American Sociological Review* 62:94–112.

Nadeau, Richard, and Christopher J. Fleury. 1995. "Gains linguistiques anticipés et appui à la souveraineté du Québec." *Canadian Journal of Political Science* 28:35–50.

Nadeau, Richard, Pierre Martin, and André Blais. 1999. "Attitude towards Risk-Taking and Individual Choice in the Quebec

Referendum on Sovereignty." *British Journal of Political Science* 29:523–39.

Nagel, Joane, and Susan Olzak. 1982. "Ethnic Mobilization in New and Old States: An Extension of the Competition Model." *Social Problems* 30:127–43.

Nielsen, François. 1985. "Towards a Theory of Ethnic Solidarity in Modern Societies." *American Sociological Review* 50:133–49.

Oberschall, Anthony. 1973. *Social Conflict and Social Movements.* Englewood Cliffs, NJ: Prentice-Hall.

– 1975. "The Controversy over Social Psychological and Social Structural Explanations of Revolutionary Phenomenon." Paper read at the American Sociological Association Meetings, San Francisco.

– 1978a. "Theories of Social Conflict." *Annual Review of Sociology* 4:291–315. Reprinted in Oberschall 1993.

– 1978b. "The Decline of the 1960s Social Movements." *Research in Social Movements, Conflicts, and Change* 1:257–289. Reprinted in Oberschall 1993.

– 1980. "Loosely Structured Collective Conflict: A Theory and an Application." *Research in Social Movements, Conflicts, and Change* 3:45–68.

– 1993. *Social Movements: Ideologies, Interests, and Identities.* New Brunswick: Transaction Publishers.

– 1996. "Opportunities and Framing in the Eastern European Revolts of 1989." In *Comparative Perspectives on Social Movements: Political Opportunities, Mobilizing Structures, and Cultural Framings,* edited by D. McAdam, J.D. McCarthy, and M.N. Zald, 93–121. New York: Cambridge University Press.

Offe, Claus. 1987. "Challenging the Boundaries of Institutional Politics: Social Movements since the 1960s." In *Changing the Boundaries of the Political,* edited by C.S. Maier, 63–105. Cambridge: Cambridge University Press.

Oliver, Pamela. 1980. "Rewards and Punishments as Selective Incentives for Collective Action: Theoretical Investigations." *American Journal of Sociology* 85:1356–75.

– 1984. "'If You Don't Do It, Nobody Else Will': Active and Token Contributors to Local Collective Action." *American Sociological Review* 49:601–10.

– 1989. "Bringing the Crowd Back In: The Nonorganizational Elements of Social Movements." *Research in Social Movements, Conflicts, and Change* 11:1–30.

Olson, Mancur. 1965. *The Logic of Collective Action: Public Goods and the Theory of Groups.* Cambridge, MA: Harvard University Press.

Olzak, Susan, and Suzanne Shanahan. 1996. "Deprivation and Race Riots: An Extension of Spilerman's Analysis." *Social Forces* 74:931–61.

Opp, Karl-Dieter. 1988. "Grievances and Participation in Social Movements." *American Sociological Review* 53:853–64.

– 1989. *The Rationality of Political Protest.* Boulder: Westview Press.

Orum, Anthony M. 1972. *Black Students in Protest: A Study of the Origins of the Black Student Movement.* Washington: American Sociological Association.

Paige, Jeffery M. 1971. "Political Orientation and Riot Participation." *American Sociological Review* 36:810–20.

Parkin, Frank. 1968. *Middle Class Radicalism: The Social Bases of the British Campaign for Nuclear Disarmament.* Manchester: Manchester University Press.

Passy, Florence. 2001. "Socialization, Connection, and the Structure/Agency Gap." *Mobilization* 6:173–192.

Pencavel, John H. 1970. "An Investigation into Industrial Strike Activity in Britain." *Economica* 37:239–56.

Perrow, Charles. 1979. "The Sixties Observed." In *The Dynamics of Social Movements: Resource Mobilization, Social Control and Tactics,* edited by M.N. Zald and J.D. McCarthy, 192–211. Cambridge, MA: Winthrop Publishers.

Pettigrew, Thomas F., and Robert T. Riley. 1971. "The Social Psychology of the Wallace Phenomenon." In T.F. Pettigrew, *Racially Separate or Together?* chap. 10. New York: McGraw-Hill.

Piliavin, Jane Allyn, and Hong-Wen Charng. 1990. "Altruism: A Review of Recent Theory and Research." *Annual Review of Sociology* 16:27–65.

Pinard, Maurice. 1975 [1971]. *The Rise of a Third Party: A Study in Crisis Politics.* Enlarged edition. Montreal and Kingston: McGill-Queen's University Press.

– 1980. "Self-Determination in Quebec: Loyalties, Incentives, and Constitutional Options among French-Speaking Quebecers." In *Resolving Nationality Conflicts*, edited by W.P. Davison and L. Gordenker, 140–76. New York: Praeger.

– 1997a. "Les fluctuations du mouvement indépendantiste depuis 1980." In *Un combat inachevé*, M. Pinard, R. Bernier, and V. Lemieux, chap. 4. Québec: Presses de l'Université du Québec.

– 1997b. "Les déterminants psychosociaux." In *Un combat inachevé*, M. Pinard, R. Bernier, and V. Lemieux, chap. 10. Québec: Presses de l'Université du Québec.

– 2002. "The Quebec Independence Movement." In *Political Sociology: Canadian Perspectives*, edited by D.Baer, chap. 13. Don Mills, ON: Oxford University Press.

– Forthcoming. *The Quebec Independence Movement*. Montreal and Kingston: McGill-Queen's University Press.

Pinard, Maurice, and Richard Hamilton. 1977. "The Independence Issue and the Polarization of the Electorate: The 1973 Quebec Election." *Canadian Journal of Political Science* 10:215–59.

– 1978. "The Parti Québécois Comes to Power: An Analysis of the 1976 Quebec Election." *Canadian Journal of Political Science* 11:739–75.

– 1984. "The Class Bases of the Quebec Independence Movement." *Ethnic and Racial Studies* 7:19–54.

– 1986. "Motivational Dimensions in the Quebec Independence Movement: A Test of a New Model." *Research in Social Movements, Conflicts, and Change* 9:225–80.

– 1989. "Intellectuals and the Leadership of Social Movements: Some Comparative Perspectives." *Research in Social Movements, Conflicts and Change* 11:73–107.

Pinard, Maurice, Jerome Kirk, and Donald Von Eschen. 1969. "Processes of Recruitment in the Sit-In Movement." *Public Opinion Quarterly* 33:355–69.

Piroth, Scott. 2004. "Generational Replacement, Value Shifts, and Support for a Sovereign Quebec." *Quebec Studies* 37:23–43.

Piven, Frances Fox, and Richard A. Cloward. 1979. *Poor People's Movements: Why They Succeed, How They Fail*. New York: Vintage Books.

– 1992. "Normalizing Collective Protest." In *Frontiers in Social Movement Theory*, edited by A.D. Morris and C.M. Mueller, 301–25. New Haven: Yale University Press.

Polletta, Francesca, and James M. Jasper. 2001. "Collective Identity and Social Movements." *Annual Review of Sociology* 27:283–305.

Ransford, H. Edward. 1968. "Isolation, Powerlessness, and Violence: A Study of Attitudes and Participation in the Watts Riot." *American Journal of Sociology* 73:581–91.

Redding, Kent. 1992. "Failed Populism: Movement-Party Disjuncture in North Carolina, 1890 to 1900." *American Sociological Review* 57:340–52.

Roefs, Marlene, Bert Klandermans, and Johan Olivier. 1998. "Protest Intentions on the Eve of South Africa's First Nonracial Elections: Optimists Look beyond Injustice." *Mobilization* 3:51–68.

Rudé, George. 1964. *The Crowd in History: A Study of Popular Disturbances in France and England, 1730–1848*. New York: Wiley.

Rule, James B. 1988. *Theories of Civil Violence*. Berkeley: University of California Press.

Rule, James B., and Charles Tilly. 1975. "Political Process in Revolutionary France, 1830–1832." In *1830 in France*, edited by J.M.Merriman, 41–85. New York: New Viewpoints.

Sambanis, Nicholas. 2001. "Do Ethnic and Nonethnic Civil Wars Have the Same Causes?" *Journal of Conflict Resolution* 45:259–82.

Searles, Ruth, and J. Allen Williams, Jr. 1962. "Negro College Students' Participation in Sit-Ins." *Social Forces* 40:215–20.

Sears, David O., and John B. McConahay. 1970. "Racial Socialization, Comparison Levels, and the Watts Riot." *Journal of Social Issues* 26:121–40.

Shorey, John. 1977. "Time Series Analysis of Strike Frequency." *British Journal of Industrial Relations* 15:63–75.

Shorter, Edward, and Charles Tilly. 1974. *Strikes in France, 1830–1968*. New York: Cambridge University Press.

Simon, Bernd, Michael Loewy, Stefan Stürmer, Ulrike Weber, Peter Freytag, Corinna Habig, Claudia Kempmeier, and Peter Spahlinger. 1998. "Collective Identification and Social Movement Participation." *Journal of Personality and Social Psychology* 74:646–58.

Skeels, Jack. 1974. "Comparative Analysis of Strike Determinants." *Journal of Economics and Business* 26:108–14.

Skogstad, Grace. 1980. "Agrarian Protest in Alberta." *Canadian Review of Sociology and Anthropology* 17:55–73.

Smelser, Neil. 1963. *Theory of Collective Behavior*. New York: The Free Press.

Smith, Douglas A. 1972. "The Determinants of Strike Activity in Canada." *Industrial Relations* 27:663–78.

Smith, Heather J., and Daniel J. Ortiz. 2002. "Is It Just Me? The Different Consequences of Personal and Group Relative Deprivation." In *Relative Deprivation: Specification, Development, and Integration,* edited by I. Walker and H..J. Smith, 91–115. New York: Cambridge University Press.

Smith, Michael R. 1979. "Institutional Setting and Industrial Conflict in Quebec." *American Journal of Sociology* 85:109–34.

– 1981. "Industrial Conflict in Postwar Ontario, or One Cheer for the Woods Report." *Canadian Review of Sociology and Anthropology* 18:370–92.

Snow, David A. 2004. "Framing Processes, Ideology, and Discursive Fields." In *The Blackwell Companion to Social Movements*, edited by D.A. Snow, S.A. Soule, and H. Kriesi, 380–412. Malden, MA: Blackwell Publishing.

Snow, David A., and Robert D. Benford. 1988. "Ideology, Frame Resonance, and Participant Mobilization." *International Social Movement Research* 1:197–217.

– 1992. "Master Frames and Cycles of Protest." In *Frontiers in Social Movement Theory*, edited by A.D. Morris and C.M. Mueller, 133–55. New Haven: Yale University Press.

Snow, David A., D.M. Cress, L. Downey, and A.W. Jones. 1998. "Disrupting the 'Quotidian': Reconceptualizing the Relationship between Breakdown and the Emergence of Collective Action." *Mobilization* 3:1–22.

Snow, David A., and Doug McAdam. 2000. "Identity Work Processes in the Context of Social Movements: Clarifying the Identity/Movement Nexus." In *Self, Identity, and Social Movements,* edited by S. Stryker, T.J. Owens, and R.W. White, 41–67. Minneapolis: University of Minnesota Press.

Snow, David A., and Pamela E. Oliver. 1995. "Social Movements and Collective Behaviour: Social Psychological Dimensions and

Considerations." In *Sociological Perspectives on Social Psychology*, edited by K.S. Cook, G.A. Fine, and J.S. House, 571–99. Boston: Allyn and Bacon.

Snow, David A., E. Burke Rochford, Jr., Steven K. Worden, and Robert D. Benford. 1986. "Frame Alignment Processes, Micromobilization, and Movement Participation." *American Sociological Review* 51:464–81.

Snow, David A., Sarah A. Soule, and Daniel M. Cress. 2005. "Identifying the Precipitants of Homeless Protest across 17 US Cities, 1980 to 1990." *Social Forces* 83:1183–1210.

Snyder, David. 1975. "Institutional Setting and Industrial Conflict: Comparative Analyses of France, Italy, and the United States." *American Sociological Review* 40:259–78.

– 1977. "Early North American Strikes: A Reinterpretation." *Industrial and Labor Relations Review* 30:325–41.

– 1978. "Collective Violence: A Research Agenda and Some Strategic Considerations." *Journal of Conflict Resolution* 22:499–534.

– 1979. "Collective Violence Processes: Implication for Disaggregated Theory and Research." *Research in Social Movements, Conflicts and Change* 2:35–61.

Snyder, David, and Charles Tilly. 1972. "Hardship and Collective Violence in France, 1830–1960." *American Sociological Review* 37:520–32.

– 1974. "On Debating and Falsifying Theories of Collective Violence." *American Sociological Review* 39:610–13.

Somers, Robert H. 1965. "The Mainsprings of the Rebellion: A Survey of Berkeley Students in November, 1964." In *The Berkeley Student Revolt: Facts and Interpretations*, edited by S.M. Lipset and S.S. Wolin, 530–57. Garden City, NY: Doubleday.

Spilerman, Seymour. 1970. "The Causes of Racial Distrubances: A Comparison of Alternative Explanations." *American Sociological Review* 35:627–49.

– 1971. "The Causes of Racial Disturbances: Tests of an Explanation." *American Sociological Review* 36:427–42.

– 1976. "Structural Characteristics of Cities and the Severity of Racial Disorder." *American Sociological Review* 41:771–93.

Staggenborg, Suzanne, and Josée Lecomte. 2009. "Social Movement Campaigns: Mobilization and Outcomes in the Montreal Women's Movement Community." *Mobilization* 14:163–80.

Staggenborg, Suzanne, and Verta Taylor. 2005. "Whatever Happened to the Women's Movement?" *Mobilization* 10:37–52.

Steedly, Homer R., and John W. Foley. 1979. "The Success of Protest Groups: Multivariate Analysis." *Social Science Research* 8:1–15.

Stein, Michael B. 1973. *The Dynamics of Right-Wing Protest: A Political Analysis of Social Credit in Quebec*. Toronto: University of Toronto Press.

Steinberg, Marc W. 2005. "Capitalist Law, Relations of Production and Exploitation, and Structured Possibilities for Contention, or Using Three Tillys to Make One Argument." In *Economic and Political Contention in Comparative Perspective*, edited by M. Kousis and C. Tilly, 33–47. Boulder: Paradigm Publishers.

Stinchcombe, Arthur L. 1975. "Social Structure and Politics." In *Handbook of Political Science*, edited by F. Greenstein and N.W. Polsby, 557–662. Reading, MA: Addison-Wesley.

Stürmer, Stefan, Bernd Simon, and Michael Loewy. 2003. "The Dual-Pathway Model of Social Movement Participation: The Case of the Fat Acceptance Movement." *Social Psychology Quarterly* 66:71–82.

Tarrow, Sidney. 1989a. *Democracy and Disorder: Protest and Politics in Italy 1965–1975*. Oxford: Clarendon Press.

– 1989b. *Struggle, Politics, and Reform*. Western Societies Program, Occasional Paper No. 21, Center for International Studies, Cornell University.

– 1994. *Power in Movement*. New York: Cambridge University Press.

– 1996. "States and Opportunities: The Political Structuring of Social Movements." In *Comparative Perspectives on Social Movements: Political Opportunities, Mobilizing Structures, and Cultural Framings*, edited by D. McAdam, J.D. McCarthy, and M.N. Zald, 41–61. New York: Cambridge University Press.

– 1998. *Power in Movement*. Rev. ed. New York: Cambridge University Press.

– 2001. "Silence and Voice in the Study of Contentious Politics: Introduction." In *Silence and Voice in the Study of Contentious Politics*, edited by R.R. Aminzade et al., 1–13. New York: Cambridge University Press.

Taylor, Verta. 1989. "Social Movement Continuity: The Women's Movement in Abeyance." *American Sociological Review* 54:761–75.

- 1995. "Watching for Vibes: Bringing Emotions into the Study of Feminist Organizations." In *Feminist Organizations,* edited by M.M Ferree and P.Y. Martin, 223–33. Philadelphia: Temple University Press.
- 2010. "Culture, Identity, and Emotions: Studying Social Movements As If People Really Matter." *Mobilization* 15:113–34.

Taylor, Verta, Katrina Kimport, Nella van Dyke, and Ellen Ann Andersen. 2009. "Culture and Mobilization: Tactical Repertoires, Same-Sex Weddings, and the Impact of Gay Activism." *American Sociological Review* 74:865–90.

Taylor, Verta, and Leila J. Rupp. 2002. "Loving Internationalism: The Emotion Culture of Transnational Women's Organizations, 1888–1945." *Mobilization* 7:141–58.

Taylor, Verta, and Nancy E. Whittier. 1992. "Collective Identity in Social Movement Communities." In *Frontiers in Social Movement Theory*, edited by A.D. Morris and C.M. Mueller, 104–29. New Haven: Yale University Press.

Tilly, Charles. 1973. "Does Modernization Breed Revolution." *Comparative Politics* 5:425–47.
- 1975. "Revolutions and Collective Violence." In *Handbook of Political Science*, vol. 3, edited by F. I. Greenstein and N. Polsby, 483–55. Reading, MA: Addison-Wesley.
- 1978. *From Mobilization to Revolution*. Reading, MA: Addison-Wesley.
- 1981. "Introduction." In *Class Conflict and Collective Action*, edited by L.A. Tilly and C. Tilly, 13–25. Beverly Hills: Sage Publications.
- 1986. *The Contentious French*. Cambridge, MA: Harvard University Press.

Tilly, Charles, Louise Tilly, and Richard Tilly. 1975. *The Rebellious Century 1830–1930*. Cambridge: Harvard University Press.

Tilly, Charles, and Sidney Tarrow. 2007. *Contentious Politics*. Boulder: Paradigm Publishers.

Touraine, Alain. 1985. "An Introduction to the Study of Social Movements." *Social Research* 52:749–87.

Turner, Ralph H. 1981. "Collective Behavior and Resource Mobilization as Approaches to Social Movements: Issues and Continuities." *Research in Social Movements, Conflicts and Change* 4:1–24.

Turner, Ralph H., and Lewis M. Killian. 1957, 1972, 1987. *Collective Behaviour*, 1st, 2d, and 3d eds. Englewood Cliffs, NJ: Prentice-Hall.

Useem, Bert. 1980. "Solidarity Model, Breakdown Model, and the Boston Anti-Busing Movement." *American Sociological Review* 45:357–69.

– 1985. "Disorganization and the New Mexico Prison Riot of 1980." *American Sociological Review* 50:677–88.

– 1998. "Breakdown Theories of Collective Action." *Annual Review of Sociology* 24:215–38.

Van Dyke, Nella, and Sarah A. Soule. 2002. "Structural Social Change and the Mobilizing Effect of Threat: Explaining Levels of Patriot and Militia Organizing in the United States." *Social Problems* 49:497–520.

Van Stekelenburg, Jacquelein, and Bert Klandermans. 2007. "Individuals in Movements: A Social Psychology of Contention." In *Handbook of Social Movements across Disciplines*, edited by B. Klandermans and C. Roggeband, 156–204. New York: Springer.

Van Zomeren, Martijn, Russell Spears, Agneta H. Fisher, and Colin Wayne Leach. 2004. "Put Your Money Where Your Mouth Is! Explaining Collective Action Tendencies through Group-Based Anger and Group Efficacy." *Journal of Personality and Social Psychology* 87:649–64.

Von Eschen, Donald. 1989. "Laying the Foundations for a Grammar of Motives: An Analytical Delineation of Competing Theories of the Social Psychology of Recruitment to Social Movements." McGill University, Montreal. Unpublished manuscript.

Von Eschen, Donald, Jerome Kirk, and Maurice Pinard. 1969. "The Disintegration of the Negro Non-Violent Movement." *Journal of Peace Research* 6:215–34.

– 1971. "The Organizational Substructure of Disorderly Politics." *Social Forces* 49:529–44.

Walsh, Edward J. 1981. "Resource Mobilization and Citizen Protest in Communities around Three Mile Island." *Social Problems* 29:1–21.

Walsh, Edward J., and Rex H. Warland. 1983. "Social Movement Involvement in the Wake of a Nuclear Accident: Activists and Free Riders in the TMI Area." *American Sociological Review* 48:764–80.

Walsh, William D. 1975. "Economic Conditions and Strike Activity in Canada." *Industrial Relations* 14:45–54.

Wanderer, James J. 1969. "An Index of Riot Severity and Some Correlates." *American Journal of Sociology* 74:500–5.

White, Robert W. 1989. "From Peaceful Protest to Guerrilla War: Micromobilization of the Provisional Irish Republican Army." *American Journal of Sociology* 94:1277–1302.

Willer, Robb. 2009. "Groups Reward Individual Sacrifices: The Status Solution to the Collective Action Problem." *American Sociological Review* 74:23–43.

Wimmer, Andreas, Lars-Erik Cederman, and Brian Min. 2009. "Ethnic Politics and Armed Conflict: A Configurational Analysis of a New Global Data Set." *American Sociological Review* 74: 316–37.

Wolfinger, Raymond E., Barbara Kaye Wolfinger, Kenneth Prewitt, and Sheilah Rosenback. 1964. "America's Radical Right : Politics and Ideology." In *Ideology and Discontent,* edited by D.E. Apter, 262–93. New York: Free Press.

Wood, James L. 1974. *The Sources of American Student Activism.* Lexington, MA: Heath and Co.

Young, R.A., and Shirley M. Forsyth. 1991. "Leaders' Communications in Public-Interest and Material-Interest Groups." *Canadian Journal of Political Science* 24:525–40.

Zald, Mayer N. 1996. "Culture, Ideology, and Strategic Framing." In *Comparative Perspectives on Social Movements: Political Opportunities, Mobilizing Structures, and Cultural Framings,* edited by D. McAdam, J.D. McCarthy, and M.N. Zald, 261–74. New York: Cambridge University Press.

Zald, Mayer N., and John D. McCarthy. 2002. "The Resource Mobilization Research Program: Progress, Challenge, and Transformation." In *New Directions in Contemporary Sociological Theory,* edited by J. Berger and M. Zelditch, 147–71. Lanham, MD: Rowman and Litlefield.

Zeitlin, Maurice. 1967. *Revolutionary Politics and the Cuban Working Class.* Princeton: Princeton University Press.

Index